Foreward

Unleash Your Creative Potential: A Comprehensive Guide to the World of *Digital* Printing

In today's fast-paced *digital* age, the world of printing has undergone a revolutionary transformation. *Digital* printing has emerged as a powerful tool, empowering individuals and businesses alike to bring their creative visions to life.

"The Rise of *Digital* Printing" delves into the exciting world of *digital* printing, exploring its history, evolution, and the myriad opportunities it presents. From personalized invitations to high-quality business cards, *digital* printing has revolutionized the way we approach *design* and *production*.

"Identifying Your Niche" guides you in discovering your unique niche within the printing industry. Whether you're passionate about custom t-shirts, fine art prints, or eco-friendly packaging, understanding your target market and tailoring your offerings accordingly is key to success.

"Business Plan Essentials" provides a solid foundation for your printing venture. Learn how to develop a comprehensive business plan that outlines your goals, target market, *financial* projections, and marketing strategies.

"Understandin Your Medium" takes you on a deep dive into the essential elements of printing. From paper types and finishes to ink formulations and printing techniques, this section equips you with the knowledge to make informed decisions.

"Setting Up Your Business" walks you through the practical steps of establishing your printing business. Learn about essential *equipment*, software, and legal considerations.

"Marketing and Sales" explores effective marketing strategies to attract and retain customers. From *building* a strong brand identity to leveraging *social* media and online advertising, this section empowers you to reach your target audience.

"Quality Control and Troubleshooting" emphasizes the importance of maintaining high-quality standards. Learn how to calibrate colors, troubleshoot print defects, and ensure proper packaging and shipping.

"Appendix" offers valuable resources, including a glossary of printing terms, a list of suppliers, a sample business plan, and *financial* projections.

Whether you're a budding entrepreneur or an experienced *designer*, this book is your ultimate guide to mastering the art and science of *digital* printing.

Table of Contents

Introduction

- The Rise of Digital Printing
- Identifying Your Niche
- Business Plan Essentials

Understanding Your Medium

- **Paper:**
    - Paper Weights and Grades
    - Paper Finishes and Textures
    - Specialty Papers
- **Ink:**
    - Ink Types and Their Applications
    - Color Profiles and Gamut
- **Stickers:**
    - Sticker Materials and Adhesives
    - Die-Cut and Kiss-Cut Stickers
    - Sticker Finishes and Laminations

Printing Techniques

- **Digital Printing:**
    - How Digital Printing Works
    - Pros and Cons of Digital Printing
    - Popular Digital Printing Methods (Inkjet, Laser, Toner)
- **Offset Printing:**
    - The Offset Printing Process
    - When to Choose Offset Printing
    - Pros and Cons of Offset Printing
- **Screen Printing:**
    - Screen Printing Basics
    - Screen Printing Techniques and Applications
    - Pros and Cons of Screen Printing

Setting Up Your Business

- **Equipment and Supplies:**
    - Essential Printing Equipment
    - Sourcing Reliable Suppliers
    - Inventory Management
- **Software and Design Tools:**
    - Design Software Essentials
    - Color Management and Proofing
    - File Formats for Printing
- **Legal and Financial Considerations:**
    - Business Licenses and Permits
    - Insurance
    - Taxes and Accounting

Marketing and Sales

- **Branding and Identity:**
    - Creating a Strong Brand Identity
    - Designing Effective Marketing Materials
- **Online Presence:**
    - Building a Website
    - Social Media Marketing
    - SEO and Online Advertising
- **Customer Acquisition and Retention:**
    - Sales and Marketing Strategies
    - Customer Service
    - Building Long-Term Relationships

Quality Control and Troubleshooting

- **Color Calibration and Management**
    - Maintaining Consistent Color
    - Troubleshooting Color Issues
- **Print Quality and Finishing**
    - Ensuring High-Quality Prints
    - Common Print Defects and Solutions
- **Packaging and Shipping**
    - Proper Packaging Techniques

- Shipping Carriers and Services

Appendix

- Glossary of Printing Terms
- Resources and Suppliers
- Sample Business Plan
- Financial Projections

Conclusion

The Rise of Digital Printing

Have you ever wondered how your favorite book or magazine got printed? Well, it's likely thanks to digital printing! This amazing technology has revolutionized the way we print things, making it faster, cheaper, and more personalized than ever before.

What is Digital Printing?

Unlike traditional printing methods, which use physical plates to transfer ink onto paper, digital printing uses computer files to directly print images onto paper. It's like having a high-tech printer that can print anything you want, from a single page to thousands of copies.

The Rise of Digital Printing

Digital printing has been growing rapidly in recent years. The industry is worth billions of dollars and is expected to continue growing at a fast pace. This growth is driven by several factors:

- **Faster Turnaround Times:** Digital printing can produce printed materials much faster than traditional methods, allowing for quicker delivery and shorter lead times.
- **Lower Costs:** Digital printing is more cost-effective, especially for short-run printing jobs. It eliminates the need for expensive plates and setup, making it a great choice for small businesses and individuals.
- **Greater Flexibility:** Digital printing offers greater flexibility in terms of design and customization. You can easily make changes to your design and print different versions without incurring additional costs.
- **On-Demand Printing:** Digital printing allows for on-demand printing, meaning you can print exactly what you need, when you need it. This reduces waste and saves money.

How Can You Take Advantage of Digital Printing?

As a reader, you can benefit from digital printing in many ways:

- **Personalized Products:** Digital printing enables the creation of personalized products, such as custom-made books, calendars, and greeting cards.
- **High-Quality Prints:** Modern digital printing technology produces high-quality prints that rival traditional printing methods.
- **Access to a Wider Range of Products:** Digital printing has made it possible to print on a wider range of materials, such as fabric, metal, and wood.
- **Lower Costs for Printed Materials:** The cost-effectiveness of digital printing has led to lower prices for books, magazines, and other printed materials.

The Future of Digital Printing

The future of digital printing looks bright. As technology continues to advance, we can expect to see even more innovative and exciting applications of digital printing. From 3D printing to personalize packaging, the possibilities are endless. Identifying Your Niche: A Crucial Step in Starting a Digital Printing Business

Understanding Your Niche

Before diving into the world of digital printing, it's crucial to identify your niche. A niche is a specific segment of the market that you'll target with your products and services. By focusing on a niche, you can better understand your target audience, tailor your offerings to their specific needs, and stand out from the competition.

Why is Niche Specialization Important?

- **Targeted Marketing:** A niche allows you to target your marketing efforts more effectively. You can tailor your messaging and promotions to the specific needs and interests of your target audience.
- **Competitive Advantage:** By focusing on a niche, you can become an expert in your field. This expertise can give you a competitive edge over generalist printers.
- **Higher Profit Margins:** Niche markets often have higher profit margins, as you can charge premium prices for specialized products and services.
- **Stronger Brand Identity:** A niche helps you develop a strong brand identity. By focusing on a specific area, you can create a unique brand image that resonates with your target audience.

How to Identify Your Niche

1. **Passion and Expertise:** Start by considering your passions and areas of expertise. What are you interested in? What are you good at?

2. **Market Research:** Conduct thorough market research to identify potential niches. Look for gaps in the market, underserved segments, and emerging trends.
3. **Target Audience Analysis:** Once you've identified a potential niche, analyze your target audience. Understand their demographics, psychographics, and specific needs.
4. **Competitive Analysis:** Assess the competition in your chosen niche. Identify your competitors' strengths and weaknesses, and look for opportunities to differentiate yourself.
5. **Financial Considerations:** Consider the financial implications of your niche. Evaluate the potential revenue and profitability of your chosen niche.

Niche Ideas for Digital Printing Businesses

Here are some niche ideas to inspire you:

- **Wedding Invitations and Stationery:** Specialize in creating unique and personalized wedding invitations, save-the-date cards, thank-you notes, and other wedding stationery.
- **Corporate Branding and Marketing Materials:** Focus on providing high-quality printing services for businesses, including business cards, brochures, flyers, and presentation materials.
- **Fine Art Printing:** Offer high-quality printing services for artists, photographers, and galleries, specializing in fine art prints, canvas prints, and framed artwork.
- **Custom Apparel and Merchandise:** Print custom t-shirts, hats, mugs, and other merchandise for businesses, sports teams, and events.
- **Large-Format Printing:** Specialize in large-format printing for outdoor advertising, trade shows, and events.

Building a Strong Brand Identity

Once you've identified your niche, it's important to build a strong brand identity. This includes:

- **Brand Name:** Choose a memorable and relevant brand name.
- **Brand Logo:** Design a visually appealing logo that represents your brand.
- **Brand Messaging:** Develop a clear and consistent brand message.
- **Brand Voice:** Establish a unique brand voice that reflects your personality and values.

By carefully identifying and targeting your niche, you can increase your chances of success in the competitive digital printing industry.

Business Plan Essentials: A Roadmap to Success

A well-crafted business plan is a crucial tool for any entrepreneur, especially those venturing into the digital printing industry. It serves as a roadmap, outlining your business goals, strategies, and financial projections. Here are the essential components of a comprehensive business plan:

1. Executive Summary

- **Overview:** A concise overview of your business, including its mission, vision, and goals.
- **Problem and Solution:** Clearly articulate the problem your business solves and how your unique solution addresses it.
- **Target Market:** Define your target market in detail, including demographics, psychographics, and specific needs.
- **Competitive Advantage:** Highlight what sets your business apart from competitors.
- **Financial Projections:** Summarize your projected revenue, expenses, and profitability.

2. Company Description

- **Business Structure:** Detail your legal structure (sole proprietorship, partnership, LLC, corporation).
- **Mission and Vision:** Clearly state your company's mission and vision.
- **Products and Services:** Describe the specific products and services you offer.
- **Core Competencies:** Highlight your team's strengths and unique skills.

3. Market Analysis

- **Industry Analysis:** Analyze the current state of the digital printing industry, including trends, challenges, and opportunities.
- **Target Market:** Delve deeper into your target market, including their needs, preferences, and buying behavior.

- **Competitive Analysis:** Identify your direct and indirect competitors and assess their strengths and weaknesses.
- **SWOT Analysis:** Conduct a SWOT analysis (Strengths, Weaknesses, Opportunities, Threats) to identify internal and external factors affecting your business.

4. Marketing and Sales Strategy

- **Marketing Strategy:** Outline your marketing strategies, including branding, advertising, public relations, and social media marketing.
- **Sales Strategy:** Develop a sales strategy to acquire and retain customers, including sales channels, pricing, and customer relationship management.
- **Distribution Channels:** Determine how you will distribute your products and services, whether it's direct sales, online sales, or through distributors.

5. Operations Plan

- **Production Process:** Describe your production process, from order intake to delivery.
- **Supply Chain Management:** Outline your supply chain, including sourcing materials and managing inventory.
- **Quality Control:** Explain your quality control measures to ensure customer satisfaction.
- **Technology:** Discuss the technology you'll use, such as design software, printing equipment, and e-commerce platforms.

6. Financial Projections

- **Start-up Costs:** List all initial expenses, including equipment, supplies, marketing, and legal fees.
- **Revenue Projections:** Forecast your revenue based on sales forecasts and pricing.
- **Expense Budget:** Project your operating expenses, such as rent, utilities, salaries, and marketing costs.

- **Profit and Loss Statement:** Create a projected profit and loss statement.
- **Cash Flow Statement:** Forecast your cash inflows and outflows.
- **Break-Even Analysis:** Determine the point at which your revenue equals your expenses.

7. Management Team

- **Key Personnel:** Outline the roles and responsibilities of key team members.
- **Organizational Chart:** Visualize the organizational structure of your business.

By carefully crafting a comprehensive business plan, you can increase your chances of success in the competitive digital printing industry. Remember to regularly review and update your plan to adapt to changing market conditions and business needs.

Understanding Paper: A Deep Dive for Digital Printing Entrepreneurs

Paper, the Foundation of Print

Paper is the fundamental medium for digital printing. Its weight, texture, finish, and size significantly impact the final printed product's quality, feel, and overall aesthetic appeal.

Paper Weight (GSM): A Comprehensive Guide

GSM, or Grams per Square Meter, is a measure of paper weight. It directly influences the paper's thickness, stiffness, and opacity. Here's a breakdown of common GSMs and their typical uses:

- **60-80 GSM:** Lightweight papers, often used for newsprint, brochures, and flyers.
- **90-100 GSM:** Medium-weight papers, suitable for office stationery, letterheads, and envelopes.
- **100-120 GSM:** Ideal for high-quality printing, such as magazines, brochures, and booklets.
- **130-170 GSM:** Heavy-weight papers, perfect for business cards, postcards, and covers.
- **200+ GSM:** Extra-heavyweight papers, used for luxury packaging, art prints, and board games.

Paper Sizes: A Global Standard

Paper sizes are standardized internationally to ensure compatibility across different printing equipment and software. Here are the common paper sizes used in digital printing:

- **A Series:**
    - **A4 (210 x 297 mm):** The most common size, used for documents, letters, and brochures.
    - **A3 (297 x 420 mm):** Twice the size of A4, often used for posters, maps, and blueprints.

- A2 (420 x 594 mm): Twice the size of A3, used for large-format printing, such as banners and posters.
    - A1 (594 x 841 mm): Twice the size of A2, used for architectural drawings, technical illustrations, and large-format prints.
    - A0 (841 x 1189 mm): The largest standard paper size, used for technical drawings, maps, and posters.
- **B Series:**
    - B1 (1000 x 707 mm): Used for large-format printing, such as posters and banners.
    - B2 (707 x 500 mm): Used for printing magazines, books, and calendars.
    - B3 (500 x 353 mm): Used for brochures, flyers, and postcards.

Paper Finishes and Textures

The finish and texture of paper significantly impact its appearance and feel. Here are some common paper finishes:

- **Matte:** A smooth, non-glossy finish, ideal for text-heavy documents and photographs.
- **Glossy:** A shiny, reflective finish, perfect for high-quality images and vibrant colors.
- **Silk:** A balance between matte and glossy, offering a subtle sheen.
- **Uncoated:** A natural, textured finish, often used for eco-friendly printing.
- **Embossed:** A textured finish created by pressing a design into the paper.

Specialty Papers

Specialty papers offer unique characteristics and can elevate the look and feel of your printed materials. Some common specialty papers include:

- **Colored Paper:** Available in a wide range of colors, colored paper can add a touch of personality to your designs.

- **Metallic Paper:** A paper with a metallic finish, often used for luxury packaging and invitations.
- **Recycled Paper:** An eco-friendly option that reduces environmental impact.
- **Vellum:** A translucent paper with a smooth, slightly textured surface, often used for certificates and invitations.
- **Cardstock:** A thick, sturdy paper, ideal for business cards, postcards, and packaging.

By understanding the different types of paper, their weights, sizes, finishes, and textures, you can make informed decisions to create stunning printed materials that leave a lasting impression.

Ink: The Lifeblood of Printing

Ink, the colorful liquid that brings printed materials to life, plays a crucial role in the digital printing process. The type of ink used can significantly impact the final appearance and durability of a printed piece.

Ink Types and Their Applications

1. **Dye-Based Inks:**
   - **Characteristics:** Vibrant colors, fast-drying, and cost-effective.
   - **Applications:** Photo prints, posters, and other high-quality color prints.
   - **Drawback:** Less water-resistant and prone to fading over time.
2. **Pigment-Based Inks:**
   - **Characteristics:** Durable, fade-resistant, and water-resistant.
   - **Applications:** Outdoor signage, banners, and other long-lasting prints.
   - **Drawback:** Can be less vibrant than dye-based inks.
3. **UV Curable Inks:**
   - **Characteristics:** Fast-drying, scratch-resistant, and waterproof.
   - **Applications:** Packaging, labels, and other high-quality, durable prints.
   - **Drawback:** Requires specialized UV curing equipment.
4. **Latex Inks:**
   - **Characteristics:** Low odor, water-based, and environmentally friendly.
   - **Applications:** Indoor signage, posters, and canvas prints.
   - **Drawback:** Can be less vibrant than other ink types.

Color Profiles and Gamut

Color profiles are standardized sets of data that define a specific color space. They ensure accurate color reproduction across different devices and printing processes.

- **sRGB:** A standard color space used for most digital displays and web graphics.
- **Adobe RGB:** A wider color gamut than sRGB, often used for photography and high-end printing.
- **CMYK:** A color model used in printing, combining cyan, magenta, yellow, and black inks.

Color Gamut:

The color gamut refers to the range of colors that a particular device or printing process can reproduce. A wider color gamut allows for a broader range of colors, resulting in more vibrant and accurate prints.

Factors Affecting Color Accuracy:

- **Monitor Calibration:** Ensuring your monitor is calibrated correctly is essential for accurate color representation.
- **Printer Profile:** Using the correct printer profile ensures that the colors on your screen match the printed output.
- **Paper Type:** The type of paper used can affect color reproduction.
- **Ink Quality:** High-quality inks can lead to more accurate color reproduction.
- **Printing Settings:** Proper printing settings, such as ink density and color management, are crucial.

By understanding the different types of ink, color profiles, and color gamut, you can make informed decisions to achieve the best possible print results.

Ink and Color Management: A Deeper Dive

Ink: The Lifeblood of Printing

As we've discussed, ink is a critical component of the digital printing process. The type of ink used can significantly impact the final appearance, durability, and cost of a printed piece.

Key Ink Types and Their Applications:

- **Dye-based Inks:** Ideal for photo prints and other high-quality color prints. They offer vibrant colors but may fade over time, especially when exposed to light and moisture.
- **Pigment-Based Inks:** These inks are more durable and fade-resistant, making them suitable for outdoor signage, banners, and other long-lasting applications.
- **UV Curable Inks:** These inks cure instantly when exposed to UV light, resulting in highly durable and water-resistant prints. They're often used for packaging, labels, and other high-quality applications.
- **Latex Inks:** Environmentally friendly, low-odor inks that are ideal for indoor signage, posters, and canvas prints.

Color Management: Ensuring Accurate Color Reproduction

Color management is the process of ensuring consistent color reproduction across different devices and printing processes. It involves a combination of hardware, software, and techniques to achieve accurate color representation.

Key Factors in Color Management:

- **Monitor Calibration:** Calibrating your monitor ensures that the colors you see on screen accurately represent the final printed output.
- **Printer Profiles:** Printer profiles provide information about a specific printer's color capabilities, allowing for accurate color matching.

- **Proofing:** Proofing involves comparing a printed sample to a digital proof to identify any color discrepancies.
- **Ink and Paper:** The type of ink and paper used can significantly impact color reproduction.
- **Printing Settings:** Proper printing settings, such as ink density and color management, are crucial for accurate color output.

Color Gamut:

The color gamut refers to the range of colors that a particular device or printing process can reproduce. A wider color gamut allows for a broader range of colors, resulting in more vibrant and accurate prints.

Common Color Spaces:

- **sRGB:** A standard color space used for most digital displays and web graphics.
- **Adobe RGB:** A wider color gamut than sRGB, often used for photography and high-end printing.
- **CMYK:** A color model used in printing, combining cyan, magenta, yellow, and black inks.

By understanding the intricacies of ink and color management, you can produce high-quality printed materials that meet your specific needs and exceed your expectations.

Stickers: A Versatile Medium for Branding and Promotion

Stickers have evolved from simple labels to powerful marketing tools. They can be used to brand products, promote events, and express individuality. Understanding the different materials, adhesives, cutting techniques, and finishes available is crucial for creating effective and durable stickers.

Sticker Materials

The material used for a sticker significantly impacts its durability, flexibility, and overall appearance. Here are some common sticker materials:

Vinyl:

- **Durability:** Highly durable and weather-resistant.
- **Flexibility:** Can be applied to curved surfaces.
- **Applications:** Outdoor signage, vehicle decals, bumper stickers.

Paper:

- **Eco-Friendly:** Often made from recycled materials.
- **Versatility:** Suitable for various applications, including labels and stickers.
- **Applications:** Product labels, shipping labels, and promotional stickers.

Clear Vinyl:

- **Transparency:** Allows the surface underneath to show through.
- **Durability:** Weather-resistant and long-lasting.
- **Applications:** Window decals, product labels, and bumper stickers.

Holographic Vinyl:

- **Eye-Catching:** Creates a shimmering, 3D effect.
- **Durability:** Weather-resistant and long-lasting.
- **Applications:** Promotional stickers, product labels, and decorative stickers.

Adhesives

The adhesive used on a sticker determines its stickiness, removability, and durability. Here are some common adhesive types:

Permanent Adhesive:

- **Strong Bond:** Creates a long-lasting bond.
- **Difficult to Remove:** Can damage surfaces when removed.
- **Applications:** Outdoor signage, vehicle decals, and bumper stickers.

Removable Adhesive:

- **Easy Removal:** Can be removed without leaving residue.
- **Temporary Bond:** Not as durable as permanent adhesive.
- **Applications:** Promotional stickers, product labels, and event stickers.

High-Tack Adhesive:

- **Strong Initial Bond:** Sticks to a wide range of surfaces.
- **Durable:** Can withstand harsh conditions.
- **Applications:** Outdoor signage, vehicle decals, and industrial applications.

Die-Cut and Kiss-Cut Stickers

Die-cut and kiss-cut stickers are two popular cutting techniques used to create custom-shaped stickers.

Die-Cut Stickers:

- **Custom Shapes:** Can be cut into any shape or design.
- **Clean Edges:** Precise cuts without any paper backing.
- **Applications:** Brand logos, product labels, and promotional stickers.

Kiss-Cut Stickers:

- **Paper Backing:** The sticker is cut around the design, leaving it attached to a paper backing.
- **Easy Peeling:** Simple to peel and apply.
- **Applications:** Product labels, shipping labels, and promotional stickers.

Sticker Finishes and Laminations

Sticker finishes and laminations can enhance the appearance and durability of your stickers.

Finishes:

- **Matte:** A non-reflective finish that is ideal for text-heavy stickers.
- **Glossy:** A shiny, reflective finish that adds a touch of elegance.
- **Matte Laminate:** Protects the sticker from scratches and UV damage, while maintaining a matte finish.
- **Glossy Laminate:** Protects the sticker and adds a glossy sheen.

By understanding the different materials, adhesives, cutting techniques, and finishes available, you can create custom stickers that are both visually appealing and functional.

Digital Printing: A Revolution in Printing Technology

Digital printing has revolutionized the printing industry, offering a wide range of benefits over traditional printing methods. It enables on-demand printing, faster turnaround times, and greater flexibility in design and customization.

How Digital Printing Works

Digital printing involves the direct transfer of digital image data to a printing surface without the use of physical printing plates. Here's a simplified breakdown of the process:

1. **Digital File Creation:** The desired image or document is created digitally, often using software like Adobe Photoshop or Illustrator.
2. **Image Processing:** The digital file is processed to ensure optimal print quality, including color correction, image resolution, and file format conversion.
3. **Printing:** The processed image data is sent to the printer, which uses a variety of technologies to transfer the image onto the printing surface.
4. **Finishing:** The printed materials may undergo finishing processes such as cutting, folding, binding, and laminating.

Popular Digital Printing Methods

1. Inkjet Printing

- **How it Works:** Inkjet printers spray tiny droplets of ink onto the printing surface.
- **Pros:** High-quality color reproduction, versatility, and ability to print on various media.
- **Cons:** Can be slower than other digital printing methods, and ink can smudge if not dried properly.

2. Laser Printing

- **How it Works:** Laser printers use a laser beam to create an electrostatic image on a drum, which attracts toner powder. The toner is then fused to the paper using heat and pressure.
- **Pros:** High-speed printing, excellent text quality, and durability.
- **Cons:** Limited color gamut compared to inkjet printing, and higher initial cost of the printer.

3. Toner Printing

- **How it Works:** Similar to laser printing, toner printing uses toner powder to create images on paper. However, it often uses a different type of toner and printing process.
- **Pros:** High-quality color and monochrome printing, versatility, and relatively low cost per print.
- **Cons:** Can be slower than laser printing, and toner can be messy if not handled properly.

Pros and Cons of Digital Printing

Pros:

- **Faster Turnaround Times:** Digital printing eliminates the need for physical plates, allowing for quick turnaround times.
- **On-Demand Printing:** Print only what you need, reducing waste and minimizing storage costs.
- **Versatility:** Digital printing can handle a wide range of materials and print sizes.
- **Customization:** Easily customize designs and personalize printed materials.
- **Cost-Effective for Short Runs:** Digital printing is more cost-effective for short-run jobs compared to traditional printing methods.

Cons:

- **Higher Initial Costs:** Digital printing equipment can be expensive.
- **Lower Print Quality for Large-Format Printing:** Digital printing may not be suitable for large-format printing that requires high-resolution images.
- **Ink Costs:** Ink costs can add up, especially for high-volume printing.

By understanding the different types of digital printing and their advantages and disadvantages, you can make informed decisions to choose the best method for your specific printing needs.

Offset Printing: A Classic Technique with Modern Applications

Offset printing is a traditional printing technique that has been widely used for centuries. It involves transferring ink from a plate to a rubber blanket, and then onto the final printing surface. Despite the rise of digital printing, offset printing remains a popular choice for many applications due to its high quality and cost-effectiveness for large print runs.

The Offset Printing Process

1. **Platemaking:** A digital image of the desired design is transferred onto a thin metal plate.
2. **Inking:** The plate is inked, and excess ink is wiped away.
3. **Imaging:** The inked image is transferred to a rubber blanket.
4. **Printing:** The image is transferred from the blanket to the paper or other printing surface.

When to Choose Offset Printing

Offset printing is an ideal choice for:

- **Large Print Runs:** It becomes more cost-effective as the print run increases.
- **High-Quality Printing:** Offset printing can produce high-quality prints with vibrant colors and sharp details.
- **Complex Designs:** It can handle complex designs with multiple colors and intricate details.
- **Specialty Papers:** Offset printing can be used with a wide range of paper types and finishes.

Pros and Cons of Offset Printing

Pros:

- **High-Quality Prints:** Offset printing can produce high-quality prints with vibrant colors and sharp details.
- **Cost-Effective for Large Runs:** As the print run increases, the cost per unit decreases, making it a cost-effective option.
- **Versatility:** Offset printing can be used with a wide range of paper types and finishes.
- **Consistency:** Offset printing can produce consistent results, even for large print runs.

Cons:

- **High Initial Setup Costs:** The initial setup costs, including platemaking and press setup, can be high.
- **Longer Turnaround Times:** The printing process can take longer than digital printing, especially for smaller print runs.
- **Less Flexible for Short Runs:** Offset printing is less flexible for short-run jobs, as it requires more setup time and material.
- **Environmental Impact:** Offset printing can have a significant environmental impact, especially if not done sustainably.

While digital printing has gained popularity, offset printing remains a valuable tool for many printing applications. By understanding the strengths and limitations of offset printing, you can make informed decisions about when to choose this technique.

Screen Printing: A Timeless Technique

Screen printing is a versatile printing technique that involves transferring ink through a mesh screen onto a substrate. It's been used for centuries and continues to be a popular choice for various applications, from t-shirts to posters.

Screen Printing Basics

1. **Screen Preparation:** A fine mesh screen is stretched over a frame.
2. **Stencil Creation:** A stencil is created on the screen, blocking off areas where ink should not pass through.
3. **Ink Application:** Ink is applied to the screen using a squeegee.
4. **Printing:** The squeegee pushes the ink through the open areas of the stencil, transferring it onto the substrate.

Screen Printing Techniques and Applications

- **Hand-Printed Screen Printing:** A traditional method that involves manually applying ink to the screen and pulling the squeegee. It's ideal for small-scale production and custom designs.
- **Automatic Screen Printing:** A more efficient method that uses automated machines to print multiple colors and designs. It's suitable for large-scale production and consistent quality.
- **Plastisol Ink Screen Printing:** A popular technique that uses plastisol ink, which is cured with heat to create durable, vibrant prints. It's commonly used for t-shirts, bags, and other apparel.
- **Water-Based Ink Screen Printing:** An environmentally friendly option that uses water-based inks. It's suitable for a variety of substrates, including paper, fabric, and wood.

Pros and Cons of Screen Printing

Pros:

- **Durability:** Screen-printed designs are highly durable and resistant to fading and washing.
- **Vibrant Colors:** Screen printing can produce vibrant and bold colors.
- **Versatility:** It can be used on a wide range of substrates, including fabric, paper, wood, and metal.
- **Texture:** Screen printing can create unique textures and effects.
- **Cost-Effective for Large Runs:** It becomes more cost-effective as the print run increases.

Cons:

- **Higher Setup Costs:** The initial setup costs, including screen preparation and stencil creation, can be relatively high.
- **Less Suitable for Small Runs:** Screen printing is not ideal for small print runs due to the setup time and costs.
- **Limited Color Palette:** While screen printing can produce vibrant colors, the number of colors is limited by the number of screens required.
- **Environmental Impact:** Traditional screen printing processes can have a significant environmental impact due to the use of chemicals and water.

By understanding the basics of screen printing and its advantages and limitations, you can make informed decisions about when to choose this technique for your printing projects.

The Future of Screen Printing

While digital printing has gained significant popularity, screen printing remains a valuable technique for many applications. Here are some trends shaping the future of screen printing:

1. Sustainable Screen Printing

- **Eco-Friendly Inks:** Using water-based and solvent-free inks to reduce environmental impact.
- **Recycled Materials:** Utilizing recycled screens and frames.
- **Energy-Efficient Equipment:** Implementing energy-saving technologies in printing presses.

2. Digital Integration

- **Computer-to-Screen (CTS):** Using digital technology to create stencils, improving accuracy and efficiency.
- **Direct-to-Screen Printing:** Printing directly onto the screen, eliminating the need for traditional stencil-making techniques.
- **Automated Screen Printing:** Using robotic systems to automate various stages of the printing process.

3. Specialized Techniques

- **Embroidery Simulation:** Creating a raised, embroidered effect using screen printing techniques.
- **Metallic and Glitter Inks:** Adding a touch of glamour to designs.
- **Glow-in-the-Dark Inks:** Creating eye-catching designs that shine in the dark.

4. Niche Markets

- **Custom Apparel:** Printing unique designs on t-shirts, hoodies, and other apparel.

- **Home Decor:** Creating custom wall art, pillows, and other home decor items.
- **Promotional Products:** Printing branded merchandise, such as tote bags, hats, and phone cases.

By embracing sustainability, innovation, and niche markets, screen printing can continue to thrive in the years to come.

Setting Up Your Digital Printing Business: Essential Equipment and Supplies

To start a successful digital printing business, you'll need to invest in the right equipment and supplies. Here's a breakdown of the essentials:

Essential Printing Equipment

1. **Digital Printer:**
    - **Inkjet Printers:** Versatile for a wide range of applications, including photo printing, document printing, and fine art printing.
    - **Laser Printers:** Ideal for high-quality text-based documents and business graphics.
    - **Large-Format Printers:** Used for printing banners, posters, and signage.
2. **Computer System:**
    - **Powerful Processor:** A powerful processor is essential for handling complex design files and image processing.
    - **Sufficient RAM:** Adequate RAM ensures smooth operation and prevents slowdowns.
    - **Large Storage Capacity:** A large hard drive or SSD is necessary for storing design files, images, and fonts.
3. **Design Software:**
    - **Adobe Creative Suite:** Industry-standard software for graphic design, photo editing, and illustration.
    - **CorelDRAW:** A versatile graphic design software suitable for various design tasks.
4. **Finishing Equipment:**
    - **Paper Cutter:** For cutting paper to the desired size.
    - **Laminator:** For protecting printed materials with a plastic film.
    - **Binder:** For binding documents and booklets.

Sourcing Reliable Suppliers

Reliable suppliers are crucial for the success of your digital printing business. Here are some tips for sourcing reliable suppliers:

- **Research:** Research suppliers online and through industry directories.
- **Quality Assurance:** Check the quality of the products and services offered by potential suppliers.
- **Pricing:** Compare prices from different suppliers to get the best deals.
- **Reliability:** Choose suppliers with a proven track record of reliability and timely delivery.
- **Customer Service:** Good customer service is essential for resolving issues and building strong relationships.

Inventory Management

Effective inventory management is key to running a successful digital printing business. Here are some tips for managing your inventory:

- **Stock Control:** Keep track of your inventory levels to avoid stockouts and overstocking.
- **Supplier Relationships:** Build strong relationships with reliable suppliers to ensure timely deliveries.
- **Storage:** Store your inventory in a clean, dry, and secure location.
- **Quality Control:** Regularly inspect your inventory for damage and defects.
- **Inventory Software:** Use inventory management software to track stock levels, sales, and purchase orders.

By investing in the right equipment, sourcing reliable suppliers, and implementing effective inventory management strategies, you can set the foundation for a successful digital printing business.

Software and Design Tools: Essential Tools for Digital Printing

Design Software Essentials

To create stunning designs for your digital printing projects, you'll need to invest in powerful design software. Here are some of the most popular options:

1. Adobe Creative Suite:

- **Adobe Photoshop:** Industry-standard software for image editing and manipulation.
- **Adobe Illustrator:** Vector graphics software for creating logos, illustrations, and typography.
- **Adobe InDesign:** Layout and publishing software for creating brochures, magazines, and books.

2. CorelDRAW Graphics Suite:

- **CorelDRAW:** Versatile vector graphics software for illustration, layout, and typography.
- **Corel PHOTO-PAINT:** Bitmap image editing software for photo manipulation and retouching.

3. Affinity Designer and Photo:

- **Affinity Designer:** Professional vector graphic design software.
- **Affinity Photo:** Professional photo editing software.

4. Canva:

- **User-Friendly Design Tool:** Easy-to-use for creating social media graphics, presentations, and more.

Color Management and Proofing

Color management is crucial for ensuring accurate color reproduction in your printed materials. Here are some key considerations:

- **Monitor Calibration:** Calibrate your monitor to accurately display colors.
- **Color Profiles:** Use appropriate color profiles (e.g., sRGB, Adobe RGB, CMYK) for different output devices.
- **Soft Proofing:** Simulate the appearance of printed colors on your monitor.
- **Hard Proofing:** Print a physical proof to verify color accuracy.

File Formats for Printing

The choice of file format can significantly impact the quality and compatibility of your printed materials. Here are some common file formats used in digital printing:

- **PDF (Portable Document Format):** A versatile format that preserves the original formatting and layout of documents.
- **EPS (Encapsulated PostScript):** A vector graphics format used for high-quality printing.
- **TIFF (Tagged Image File Format):** A lossless image format suitable for high-resolution images.
- **JPEG (Joint Photographic Experts Group):** A compressed image format commonly used for web graphics and digital photography.
- **PNG (Portable Network Graphics):** A lossless image format that supports transparency.
- **AI (Adobe Illustrator):** A vector graphics format used for creating scalable designs.
- **PSD (Photoshop Document):** A layered image format used for editing and manipulating images.
- **Indd (InDesign Document):** A layout and publishing format used for creating multi-page documents.

When preparing files for printing, it's important to consider factors such as resolution, color mode, and file size. Consult with your printer to ensure that your files are formatted correctly for optimal print quality.

Legal and Financial Considerations for Your Digital Printing Business

Business Licenses and Permits

Before starting your digital printing business, it's crucial to obtain the necessary licenses and permits. The specific requirements may vary depending on your location, but here are some common ones:

- **Business License:** This is a general license required to operate a business.
- **Sales Tax Permit:** If you're selling products or services, you may need to collect and remit sales tax.
- **Zoning Permit:** If you're operating from a physical location, you may need a zoning permit to ensure compliance with local zoning regulations.
- **Health and Safety Permits:** If you handle hazardous materials or operate heavy machinery, you may need specific health and safety permits.
- **Environmental Permits:** Depending on your operations, you may need permits to comply with environmental regulations.

Consult with a local business attorney or a Small Business Administration (SBA) office to determine the specific licenses and permits required for your business.

Insurance

Insurance is essential to protect your business from potential risks. Consider the following types of insurance:

- **General Liability Insurance:** Covers property damage, bodily injury, and product liability.
- **Professional Liability Insurance:** Protects against claims of negligence or errors in your services.
- **Workers' Compensation Insurance:** Covers medical expenses and lost wages for employees injured on the job.

- **Property Insurance:** Protects your business property, including equipment and inventory.

Taxes and Accounting

Understanding your tax obligations and keeping accurate financial records are crucial for the success of your business. Here are some key tax considerations:

- **Income Tax:** You'll need to pay income tax on your business profits.
- **Sales Tax:** If you're selling products or services, you may need to collect and remit sales tax.
- **Property Tax:** If you own a physical location, you'll need to pay property tax.
- **Business Licenses and Permit Fees:** These fees may be considered business expenses.

Hiring an Accountant: Consider hiring an accountant to help you with:

- **Tax Planning:** To minimize your tax liability.
- **Financial Reporting:** To track your income and expenses.
- **Payroll:** To manage employee payroll and taxes.
- **Bookkeeping:** To maintain accurate financial records.

By understanding and addressing these legal and financial considerations, you can ensure the smooth operation of your digital printing business.

Marketing and Sales: Building Your Brand and Attracting Customers

Branding and Identity

A strong brand identity is essential for any business, including a digital printing business. Your brand identity should be consistent across all your marketing materials and customer interactions. Here are some key elements to consider:

- **Brand Name:** Choose a name that is memorable, relevant, and easy to pronounce.
- **Brand Logo:** Design a visually appealing logo that represents your brand and is easy to recognize.
- **Brand Colors:** Select a color palette that reflects your brand personality and evokes the desired emotions.
- **Brand Voice and Tone:** Develop a consistent tone of voice for your brand's messaging.
- **Brand Messaging:** Create a clear and concise brand message that communicates your unique value proposition.

Designing Effective Marketing Materials

Effective marketing materials can help you attract new customers and retain existing ones. Here are some tips for designing marketing materials:

- **Know Your Target Audience:** Understand your target audience's needs, preferences, and pain points.
- **Keep It Simple:** Avoid clutter and focus on a clear message.
- **Use High-Quality Images:** Invest in high-quality images to create visually appealing materials.
- **Use Strong Call-to-Action:** Encourage your audience to take action, such as visiting your website or making a purchase.
- **Consistency:** Maintain consistency in your branding across all marketing materials.

Here are some marketing materials you can create:

- **Business Cards:** A classic marketing tool that can be used to network and promote your business.
- **Brochures:** A versatile marketing tool that can be used to showcase your products and services.
- **Flyers:** A cost-effective way to promote your business and special offers.
- **Postcards:** A direct mail piece that can be used to generate leads and drive sales.
- **Social Media Graphics:** Visually appealing graphics to share on social media platforms.
- **Email Marketing:** Personalized emails to nurture leads and promote your products and services.
- **Website:** A professional website to showcase your business and attract customers online.

By focusing on your brand identity and creating effective marketing materials, you can build a strong brand and attract more customers to your digital printing business.

Online Presence: Building a Strong Digital Footprint

Building a Website

A well-designed website is essential for any business, including a digital printing business. Here are some key considerations for building a website:

1. Domain Name:

- Choose a domain name that is relevant to your business and easy to remember.
- Consider using a domain name that includes relevant keywords.

2. Web Hosting:

- Select a reliable web hosting provider that offers adequate storage and bandwidth.
- Consider factors like uptime, security, and customer support.

3. Website Design:

- **User-Friendly Design:** Create a website that is easy to navigate and visually appealing.
- **Mobile-Friendly Design:** Ensure your website is optimized for mobile devices.
- **Clear Call-to-Action:** Guide visitors to take the desired action, such as contacting you or making a purchase.
- **Fast Loading Speed:** Optimize your website for fast loading times.

4. Content Creation:

- **High-Quality Content:** Create informative and engaging content that appeals to your target audience.

- **Keyword Optimization:** Use relevant keywords to improve your website's search engine ranking.
- **Regular Updates:** Keep your website fresh by regularly adding new content.

Social Media Marketing

Social media platforms offer a powerful way to connect with your target audience and promote your business. Here are some tips for effective social media marketing:

- **Platform Selection:** Choose platforms that align with your target audience, such as Instagram, Facebook, Twitter, LinkedIn, and Pinterest.
- **Consistent Posting:** Create a consistent posting schedule to keep your audience engaged.
- **Visual Content:** Use high-quality images and videos to grab attention.
- **Engaging Content:** Share informative, entertaining, and inspiring content.
- **Social Media Advertising:** Consider using paid advertising to reach a wider audience.

SEO and Online Advertising

Search Engine Optimization (SEO) and online advertising can help you attract more traffic to your website and generate leads.

SEO:

- **Keyword Research:** Identify relevant keywords and incorporate them into your website content.
- **On-Page SEO:** Optimize your website's title tags, meta descriptions, and header tags.
- **Off-Page SEO:** Build backlinks from other websites to improve your website's authority.

Online Advertising:

- **Pay-Per-Click (PPC) Advertising:** Bid on keywords to display ads on search engine results pages.
- **Social Media Advertising:** Target specific demographics and interests with social media ads.
- **Display Advertising:** Use banner ads and other display ads to reach a wider audience.

By effectively utilizing these online marketing strategies, you can increase your brand visibility, attract new customers, and drive sales for your digital printing business.

Customer Acquisition and Retention: Building a Loyal Customer Base

Sales and Marketing Strategies

1. Direct Sales:

- **Personal Sales:** Build relationships with potential clients through face-to-face meetings and presentations.
- **Telemarketing:** Use telemarketing to reach a wider audience and generate leads.

2. Digital Marketing:

- **Search Engine Optimization (SEO):** Optimize your website to rank higher in search engine results.
- **Pay-Per-Click (PPC) Advertising:** Use paid advertising to drive traffic to your website.
- **Social Media Marketing:** Leverage social media platforms to connect with your target audience.
- **Email Marketing:** Build an email list and send targeted marketing campaigns.

3. Content Marketing:

- **Blogging:** Create informative blog posts to attract and engage your audience.
- **Video Marketing:** Produce high-quality videos to showcase your products and services.
- **Infographics:** Use visually appealing infographics to communicate complex information.

4. Partnerships and Collaborations:

- **Strategic Alliances:** Partner with complementary businesses to cross-promote each other's services.
- **Joint Ventures:** Collaborate with other businesses to create new products or services.

Customer Service

Excellent customer service is essential for building long-term relationships with your clients. Here are some tips for providing exceptional customer service:

- **Responsiveness:** Respond to customer inquiries and concerns promptly.
- **Empathy:** Show empathy and understanding for your customers' needs.
- **Problem-Solving:** Actively work to resolve any issues or complaints.
- **Proactive Communication:** Keep customers informed about the status of their orders and any potential delays.
- **Personalized Service:** Tailor your service to the individual needs of each customer.

Building Long-Term Relationships

Strong customer relationships are vital for the long-term success of your business. Here are some strategies for building lasting relationships:

- **Loyalty Programs:** Implement loyalty programs to reward repeat customers.
- **Customer Appreciation:** Show your appreciation for your customers through special offers, discounts, or personalized gifts.
- **Feedback and Surveys:** Gather feedback from your customers to improve your products and services.
- **Social Media Engagement:** Interact with your customers on social media.
- **Exceptional Service:** Consistently deliver excellent customer service to build trust and loyalty.

By focusing on these areas, you can attract new customers, retain existing ones, and build a strong reputation for your digital printing business.

Quality Control and Troubleshooting: Ensuring Color Accuracy and Print Quality

Color Calibration and Management

Color calibration and management are crucial for ensuring accurate color reproduction in your digital printing. Here are some key strategies:

1. Monitor Calibration:

- **Regular Calibration:** Calibrate your monitor regularly to ensure accurate color representation.
- **Color Calibration Tools:** Use color calibration tools to adjust your monitor's color settings.
- **Software Profiles:** Create custom color profiles for your monitor to optimize color accuracy.

2. Printer Profiles:

- **Create Custom Profiles:** Create custom printer profiles to accurately represent colors on different paper types and ink combinations.
- **Use Predefined Profiles:** Use pre-defined ICC profiles for specific printers and papers.

3. Soft Proofing:

- **Simulate Printed Colors:** Use software to simulate how colors will appear on different papers and inks.
- **Compare Digital and Physical Proofs:** Compare digital proofs to physical proofs to identify any color discrepancies.

4. Color Management Software:

- **Color Management Software:** Use color management software to control color throughout the printing process.

- **Color Correction:** Use color correction tools to adjust color balance, contrast, and saturation.

Troubleshooting Color Issues

If you encounter color issues in your printed materials, here are some troubleshooting tips:

1. Check Monitor Calibration:

- Ensure your monitor is calibrated correctly to avoid color shifts.

2. Review Printer Profiles:

- Verify that the correct printer profile is being used for the specific paper and ink combination.

3. Inspect Ink and Paper:

- Check for expired or low-quality ink.
- Ensure you're using the appropriate paper type for the desired color output.

4. Monitor Environmental Conditions:

- Temperature and humidity can affect color accuracy. Maintain a stable environment.

5. Clean Printing Equipment:

- Clean your printer regularly to prevent ink buildup and nozzle clogs.

6. Seek Professional Help:

- Consult with a color management expert for advanced troubleshooting and calibration.

By following these guidelines, you can ensure consistent color accuracy and produce high-quality printed materials.

Print Quality and Finishing

Ensuring High-Quality Prints

- **Image Resolution:** Use high-resolution images to avoid pixelation and other issues.
- **Color Mode:** Choose the appropriate color mode (RGB or CMYK) for your project.
- **File Format:** Use appropriate file formats, such as PDF, TIFF, or EPS, to preserve image quality.
- **Proofing:** Review proofs carefully to identify any errors or color discrepancies.
- **Regular Maintenance:** Keep your printing equipment clean and well-maintained.

Common Print Defects and Solutions

- **Color Mismatch:** Calibrate your monitor and printer, and use accurate color profiles.
- **Banding:** Adjust the ink density and print speed settings.
- **Streaking:** Clean the printheads and check the ink supply.
- **Blurring:** Adjust the focus and resolution settings.
- **Paper Jams:** Regularly clean the paper path and avoid using damaged paper.

Packaging and Shipping

- **Protective Packaging:** Use appropriate packaging materials to protect your printed products during shipping.
- **Labeling:** Clearly label packages with the recipient's address and any special handling instructions.
- **Shipping Carrier:** Choose a reliable shipping carrier that offers tracking and insurance.
- **Shipping Costs:** Calculate shipping costs accurately and pass them on to the customer or absorb them into your pricing.

By following these guidelines, you can ensure that your printed materials are of the highest quality and arrive at their destination in perfect condition.

Additional Strategies for Customer Acquisition and Retention

Referral Programs

- **Incentivize Referrals:** Offer rewards or discounts to customers who refer new business.
- **Track Referrals:** Use a referral tracking system to monitor the effectiveness of your program.
- **Personalized Thank-You Notes:** Send personalized thank-you notes to both the referrer and the referred customer.

Customer Feedback and Surveys

- **Gather Feedback:** Use surveys, online reviews, and customer feedback forms to collect valuable insights.
- **Act on Feedback:** Implement changes based on customer feedback to improve your products and services.
- **Customer Satisfaction Surveys:** Conduct regular surveys to measure customer satisfaction.

Upselling and Cross-Selling

- **Upselling:** Encourage customers to purchase higher-value products or services.
- **Cross-Selling:** Offer complementary products or services to increase the average order value.
- **Bundling:** Package products and services together to create attractive offers.

Community Involvement

- **Local Events:** Sponsor or participate in local events to increase brand visibility.
- **Charitable Donations:** Support local charities to build goodwill and positive brand associations.

- **Volunteer Work:** Encourage your employees to volunteer in the community.

Customer Retention Strategies

- **Personalized Marketing:** Tailor your marketing messages to individual customer preferences.
- **Exclusive Offers:** Provide exclusive discounts and promotions to loyal customers.
- **Customer Loyalty Programs:** Reward loyal customers with points, discounts, or free products.
- **Exceptional Customer Service:** Consistently deliver excellent customer service to build trust and loyalty.

By implementing these strategies, you can strengthen your customer relationships, increase customer satisfaction, and drive long-term growth for your digital printing business.

Additional Strategies for Online Marketing

Email Marketing

- **Build an Email List:** Collect email addresses from website visitors and customers.
- **Personalized Emails:** Tailor your email content to the interests of your subscribers.
- **Regular Newsletters:** Send regular newsletters with updates, promotions, and valuable content.
- **Automated Email Campaigns:** Set up automated email campaigns for welcome messages, abandoned cart reminders, and post-purchase follow-ups.

Content Marketing

- **Blogging:** Create informative and engaging blog posts to attract organic traffic.
- **Video Marketing:** Produce high-quality videos to showcase your products and services.

- **Infographics:** Use visually appealing infographics to explain complex topics.
- **Guest Posting:** Contribute guest posts to other websites to increase your brand visibility.

Local SEO

- **Google My Business:** Claim and optimize your Google My Business listing.
- **Local Directories:** List your business on local directories like Yelp and Yellow Pages.
- **Online Reviews:** Encourage satisfied customers to leave positive reviews.

Social Media Advertising

- **Targeted Advertising:** Use social media advertising to reach specific demographics and interests.
- **Retargeting:** Show ads to people who have visited your website but haven't made a purchase.
- **Influencer Marketing:** Partner with influencers in your industry to promote your products and services.

By combining these strategies, you can create a comprehensive online marketing plan that will help you attract new customers, build brand awareness, and drive sales for your digital printing business.

Online Presence and Digital Marketing

In today's digital age, having a strong online presence is crucial for any business, including a digital printing business. Here are some strategies to enhance your online visibility:

Building a Strong Website

- **User-Friendly Design:** Create a website that is easy to navigate and visually appealing.
- **Mobile-Friendly:** Ensure your website is optimized for mobile devices.
- **Clear Call-to-Action:** Guide visitors to take the desired action, such as contacting you or making a purchase.
- **SEO Optimization:** Use relevant keywords to improve your website's search engine ranking.
- **Content Marketing:** Create high-quality content, such as blog posts and articles, to attract and engage your audience.

Social Media Marketing

- **Platform Selection:** Choose social media platforms that align with your target audience.
- **Consistent Posting:** Share engaging content regularly to keep your audience interested.
- **Visual Content:** Use high-quality images and videos to grab attention.
- **Community Engagement:** Interact with your audience through comments, likes, and shares.
- **Paid Advertising:** Consider using paid advertising to reach a wider audience.

Email Marketing

- **Build an Email List:** Collect email addresses from customers and potential clients.

- **Personalized Emails:** Send targeted emails to specific segments of your audience.
- **Promotional Offers:** Use email marketing to promote special offers and discounts.
- **Newsletter:** Share industry news, tips, and company updates.

Local SEO

- **Google My Business:** Claim and optimize your Google My Business listing.
- **Local Directories:** List your business on local directories like Yelp and Yellow Pages.
- **Online Reviews:** Encourage satisfied customers to leave positive reviews on Google and other platforms.

By effectively utilizing these digital marketing strategies, you can attract new customers, build brand awareness, and drive sales for your digital printing business.

Financial Considerations for Your Digital Printing Business

Understanding Your Finances

A solid understanding of your finances is crucial for the success of your digital printing business. Here are some key financial considerations:

Startup Costs

- **Equipment:** Digital printers, cutting machines, laminators, and other necessary equipment.
- **Software:** Design software, RIP software, and business management software.
- **Supplies:** Paper, ink, toner, and other consumables.
- **Rent or Lease:** If you have a physical location, you'll need to factor in rent or lease payments.
- **Utilities:** Electricity, water, and internet.
- **Insurance:** General liability, property, and workers' compensation insurance.
- **Licenses and Permits:** Fees associated with obtaining necessary licenses and permits.
- **Marketing and Advertising:** Costs for creating marketing materials and advertising your business.
- **Legal Fees:** Fees for consulting with an attorney to set up your business.

Ongoing Costs

- **Supplies:** Continual purchase of paper, ink, toner, and other consumables.
- **Equipment Maintenance:** Regular maintenance and repairs for your printing equipment.
- **Software Licenses and Updates:** Keeping your software up-to-date.
- **Employee Salaries and Benefits:** If you have employees, you'll need to pay salaries, taxes, and benefits.

- **Rent or Lease:** Ongoing costs for your physical location.
- **Utilities:** Electricity, water, and internet.
- **Insurance:** Regular payments for insurance premiums.
- **Marketing and Advertising:** Ongoing costs for marketing and advertising campaigns.
- **Accounting and Taxes:** Fees for accounting services and tax preparation.

Pricing Your Services

When pricing your services, consider the following factors:

- **Cost of Goods Sold (COGS):** The direct costs of producing your products, including materials and labor.
- **Operating Expenses:** Indirect costs, such as rent, utilities, and salaries.
- **Desired Profit Margin:** The profit you want to make on each product or service.
- **Competition:** Research your competitors' pricing to stay competitive.
- **Value-Based Pricing:** Consider the value you provide to your customers and charge accordingly.

By carefully considering these financial factors, you can make informed decisions and ensure the long-term success of your digital printing business.

Additional Considerations for Digital Printing

Print Finishing Techniques

Print finishing techniques can significantly enhance the appearance and durability of your printed materials. Here are some popular techniques:

- **Laminating:** Applying a protective film to the surface of the printed material.
- **Die-Cutting:** Cutting the paper or cardstock into custom shapes.
- **Embossing and Debossing:** Creating raised or recessed designs on the paper surface.
- **Foil Stamping:** Adding metallic or colored foil to create a luxurious look.
- **Perforation:** Creating perforated lines to allow for easy tearing.
- **Numbering and Barcoding:** Adding sequential numbers or barcodes to printed materials.

Sustainability in Digital Printing

- **Eco-Friendly Inks:** Using soy-based and vegetable-based inks to reduce environmental impact.
- **Recycled Paper:** Choosing recycled paper options to minimize waste.
- **Energy-Efficient Equipment:** Investing in energy-efficient printers and other equipment.
- **Waste Reduction:** Implementing strategies to reduce paper waste, such as double-sided printing and efficient workflow.

Quality Control in Digital Printing

- **Color Calibration:** Regularly calibrating your monitors and printers to ensure accurate color reproduction.

- **Proofing:** Reviewing proofs carefully to identify any errors or inconsistencies.
- **Quality Assurance:** Implementing quality control checks throughout the printing process.
- **Customer Communication:** Clearly communicating with clients to ensure their expectations are met.

By understanding the various aspects of digital printing, from software and hardware to design and finishing techniques, you can create high-quality printed materials that leave a lasting impression.

Setting Up Your Digital Printing Business: A Deeper Dive

Essential Printing Equipment

In addition to the basic equipment mentioned earlier, consider these additional tools and equipment:

- **Color Calibrator:** Ensures accurate color reproduction across different devices.
- **Cutting Plotter:** For precise cutting of vinyl, adhesive films, and other materials.
- **Heat Press:** For transferring designs onto garments and other materials.
- **Finishing Machines:** Including folders, binders, and laminators.
- **Software:** Design software (Adobe Creative Suite, CorelDRAW), RIP software (Raster Image Processor), and printer driver software.

Sourcing Reliable Suppliers

When sourcing supplies, consider the following factors:

- **Quality:** Ensure that the supplies meet your quality standards.
- **Cost:** Compare prices from different suppliers to get the best deals.
- **Reliability:** Choose suppliers with a good track record of timely delivery and customer service.
- **Sustainability:** Consider eco-friendly options, such as recycled paper and soy-based inks.

Inventory Management

Effective inventory management is crucial for the smooth operation of your business. Here are some strategies to consider:

- **Just-in-Time Inventory:** Minimize inventory levels by ordering supplies as needed.
- **Barcode Scanning:** Use barcode scanners to track inventory levels and streamline the checkout process.
- **Inventory Software:** Utilize inventory management software to automate tasks and generate reports.
- **Regular Stock Takes:** Conduct regular physical inventory counts to verify stock levels.
- **Quality Control:** Implement quality control measures to ensure that your inventory is free from defects.

By carefully selecting equipment, sourcing reliable suppliers, and implementing effective inventory management strategies, you can lay the foundation for a successful digital printing business. In the next section, we'll delve into the financial aspects of starting a digital printing business.

Screen Printing Techniques: A Deeper Dive

Screen Printing Techniques

1. Hand-Printed Screen Printing:

- **Process:** A manual process where ink is applied to the screen using a squeegee.
- **Advantages:** High level of control, ideal for small-scale production, and unique designs.
- **Disadvantages:** Time-consuming, labor-intensive, and less consistent than automated methods.

2. Automatic Screen Printing:

- **Process:** Uses automated machines to print multiple colors and designs.
- **Advantages:** High-speed production, consistent quality, and increased efficiency.
- **Disadvantages:** Higher initial investment, less flexibility for custom designs.

3. Plastisol Ink Screen Printing:

- **Process:** Uses plastisol ink, a PVC-based ink that cures when heated.
- **Advantages:** Durable, vibrant colors, and resistant to fading and washing.
- **Disadvantages:** Can be less environmentally friendly and requires specialized equipment.

4. Water-Based Ink Screen Printing:

- **Process:** Uses water-based inks that are more environmentally friendly.
- **Advantages:** Lower environmental impact, softer hand feel, and suitable for a variety of fabrics.

- **Disadvantages:** May not be as durable as plastisol inks, and color vibrancy can be lower.

Specialty Screen Printing Techniques

- **Discharge Printing:** Removes dye from a garment to create a design.
- **Embossing and Debossing:** Creating raised or recessed designs on the fabric.
- **Foil Printing:** Adding metallic or colored foil to the design.
- **Glow-in-the-Dark Printing:** Using special inks that glow in the dark.

Choosing the Right Screen Printing Technique

When choosing a screen printing technique, consider the following factors:

- **Design Complexity:** Simple designs are suitable for hand-printed or automatic screen printing, while complex designs may require more advanced techniques.
- **Quantity:** For small quantities, hand-printed screen printing may be sufficient. For larger quantities, automatic screen printing is more efficient.
- **Material:** The type of material being printed on will influence the choice of ink and technique.
- **Budget:** The cost of screen printing can vary depending on the technique, materials, and labor costs.

By understanding the different screen printing techniques and their applications, you can make informed decisions to create high-quality, durable, and visually appealing printed products.

The Future of Offset Printing

While digital printing has made significant strides, offset printing continues to be a valuable tool for many printing applications. Here are some trends shaping the future of offset printing:

1. Sustainable Offset Printing

- **Eco-Friendly Inks:** Using soy-based and vegetable-based inks to reduce environmental impact.
- **Recycled Paper:** Utilizing recycled paper to minimize waste.
- **Energy-Efficient Equipment:** Implementing energy-saving technologies in printing presses.

2. Digital Integration

- **Computer-to-Plate (CTP) Technology:** Eliminating film and chemicals in the platemaking process.
- **Variable Data Printing (VDP):** Personalizing printed materials with variable information, such as names, addresses, and product recommendations.
- **Digital Color Management:** Ensuring consistent color reproduction across different printing processes.

3. Specialized Printing Techniques

- **Enhanced Color Gamut:** Expanding the range of colors that can be printed.
- **Specialty Coatings:** Applying special coatings to paper to enhance its appearance and durability.
- **3D Printing:** Integrating 3D printing with offset printing to create unique and innovative products.

4. Automation and Artificial Intelligence

- **Automated Workflow:** Automating various stages of the printing process, from platemaking to finishing.

- **Predictive Maintenance:** Using AI to predict and prevent equipment failures.
- **Quality Control:** Implementing AI-powered quality control systems to ensure consistent output.

While digital printing has revolutionized the industry, offset printing remains a valuable tool for many applications. By embracing sustainable practices, integrating digital technologies, and exploring new techniques, offset printing can continue to thrive in the years to come.

Offset Printing Techniques: A Deeper Dive

Offset printing offers a variety of techniques to enhance the visual appeal and functionality of printed materials. Here are some of the most common techniques:

Sheet-Fed Offset Printing

- **How it works:** Individual sheets of paper are fed into the printing press, one at a time.
- **Applications:** Brochures, flyers, business cards, and other high-quality printed materials.
- **Advantages:** High-quality prints, versatility, and precise color control.

Web Offset Printing

- **How it works:** Large rolls of paper are fed into the printing press, and the printed sheets are cut to size.
- **Applications:** Newspapers, magazines, and books.
- **Advantages:** High-speed printing, cost-effective for large print runs, and continuous production.

Perfect Binding

- **How it works:** The pages of a book or booklet are glued together along the spine.
- **Applications:** Books, magazines, and catalogs.
- **Advantages:** Durable, professional-looking binding.

Saddle Stitching

- **How it works:** The pages of a booklet are folded and stapled together along the spine.
- **Applications:** Brochures, catalogs, and magazines.
- **Advantages:** Cost-effective and quick binding method.

Wire-O Binding

- **How it works:** The pages of a document are punched with holes and bound together with wire.
- **Applications:** Notebooks, calendars, and recipe books.
- **Advantages:** Durable and allows the book to lie flat when opened.

Coil Binding

- **How it works:** The pages of a document are punched with holes and bound together with a plastic coil.
- **Applications:** Notebooks, manuals, and training materials.
- **Advantages:** Flexible and easy to add or remove pages.

Special Effects

- **Embossing and Debossing:** Creating raised or recessed designs on the paper surface.
- **Foil Stamping:** Adding metallic or colored foil to create a luxurious look.
- **Varnishing:** Applying a protective coating to the paper surface.
- **Spot UV:** Applying a glossy coating to specific areas of the printed piece.

By understanding these techniques, you can choose the best method to achieve your desired outcome and create stunning printed materials.

The Future of Digital Printing

The digital printing industry is constantly evolving, driven by technological advancements and changing consumer demands. Here are some key trends shaping the future of digital printing:

1. 3D Printing

- **Additive Manufacturing:** Creating three-dimensional objects layer by layer.
- **Applications:** Prototyping, manufacturing, healthcare, and architecture.
- **Future Potential:** Personalized products, custom prosthetics, and organ printing.

2. Augmented Reality (AR) and Virtual Reality (VR) Printing

- **Interactive Printing:** Combining physical and digital elements to create immersive experiences.
- **Applications:** Marketing materials, education, and gaming.
- **Future Potential:** Enhanced product packaging, interactive storytelling, and virtual try-on experiences.

3. Sustainable Printing

- **Eco-Friendly Materials:** Using recycled paper and soy-based inks.
- **Energy-Efficient Equipment:** Reducing energy consumption and carbon emissions.
- **Waste Reduction:** Implementing efficient production processes and recycling programs.

4. Artificial Intelligence (AI) in Printing

- **Automated Design:** AI-powered design tools to create custom designs.
- **Predictive Maintenance:** Using AI to predict and prevent equipment failures.

- **Quality Control:** Implementing AI-powered quality control systems.

5. Personalized Printing

- **Custom Products:** Creating unique products tailored to individual preferences.
- **On-Demand Printing:** Printing products as needed, reducing waste and inventory costs.
- **Personalized Marketing:** Using data to create targeted marketing materials.

6. Flexible Electronics

- **Printed Electronics:** Printing electronic circuits directly onto flexible substrates.
- **Applications:** Wearable technology, smart packaging, and medical devices.
- **Future Potential:** Revolutionary advancements in electronics and IoT.

By embracing these emerging trends, digital printing businesses can stay ahead of the curve and continue to innovate in the years to come.

Digital Printing for Specific Applications

Digital printing offers a wide range of applications, from everyday documents to high-end marketing materials. Here are some specific applications of digital printing:

Commercial Printing

- **Brochures and Flyers:** Create eye-catching brochures and flyers to promote products and services.
- **Business Cards:** Design professional business cards to make a lasting impression.
- **Booklets and Catalogs:** Produce high-quality booklets and catalogs to showcase your products or services.
- **Posters and Banners:** Create large-format posters and banners for advertising and promotional purposes.
- **Packaging:** Design and print custom packaging for products, enhancing brand recognition and product appeal.

Personalized Printing

- **Photo Books:** Create personalized photo books to preserve memories and tell stories.
- **Greeting Cards:** Design custom greeting cards for special occasions.
- **Labels and Stickers:** Print labels and stickers for products, packaging, and promotional materials.
- **Custom Apparel:** Print custom t-shirts, hoodies, and other apparel items.

Fine Art Printing

- **Giclée Prints:** High-quality fine art prints on various media, such as canvas, paper, and metal.
- **Limited Edition Prints:** Produce limited edition prints of original artwork.

Industrial Printing

- **Packaging:** Print high-quality packaging materials, including boxes, labels, and shrink sleeves.
- **Textile Printing:** Print directly onto fabric for clothing, home decor, and other textile products.
- **Electronic Printing:** Print electronic components and circuits.

The Future of Digital Printing

Digital printing technology continues to evolve, offering new possibilities and applications. Some emerging trends in digital printing include:

- **3D Printing:** Creating three-dimensional objects from digital designs.
- **Direct-to-Garment Printing:** Printing directly onto fabric, eliminating the need for screen printing.
- **Nanoparticle Printing:** Printing at the nanoscale for advanced materials and devices.
- **Bioprinting:** Printing living cells and tissues for medical applications.

By embracing innovation and staying up-to-date with the latest trends, digital printing businesses can continue to thrive and shape the future of the printing industry.

Digital Printing Techniques: A Deeper Dive

While we've covered the basics of digital printing, let's delve deeper into specific techniques and their applications.

Inkjet Printing

Inkjet printing is a versatile technique that uses tiny nozzles to spray ink droplets onto a surface. It's widely used for:

- **Photographic Printing:** Producing high-quality photo prints with vibrant colors.
- **Document Printing:** Printing text documents, reports, and presentations.
- **Fine Art Printing:** Reproducing fine art pieces on various media, such as canvas and paper.

Types of Inkjet Printers:

- **Inkjet Printers:** Consumer-grade printers for home and office use.
- **Large-Format Inkjet Printers:** Used for printing banners, posters, and signage.
- **Industrial Inkjet Printers:** High-speed printers for packaging, labels, and direct-to-garment printing.

Laser Printing

Laser printing is a popular technique for high-quality, high-speed printing, particularly for text-based documents. It involves using a laser to create an electrostatic image on a drum, which attracts toner powder.

Applications of Laser Printing:

- **Office Documents:** Printing letters, reports, and presentations.

- **Books and Manuals:** Producing high-quality books and manuals.
- **Direct Mail:** Printing personalized direct mail pieces.

Toner Printing

Toner printing is similar to laser printing, but it uses a different type of toner and printing process. It's often used for:

- **High-Volume Printing:** Producing large quantities of printed materials.
- **Color Printing:** Creating high-quality color prints, including brochures, flyers, and catalogs.
- **Specialty Printing:** Printing on various substrates, such as cardstock, envelopes, and labels.

Emerging Digital Printing Techniques

- **3D Printing:** Creating three-dimensional objects from digital models.
- **Direct-to-Garment (DTG) Printing:** Printing directly onto fabric, eliminating the need for screen printing.
- **Wide-Format Printing:** Printing large-format graphics, such as banners, posters, and billboards.

By understanding the various digital printing techniques and their applications, you can make informed decisions to choose the best method for your specific printing needs.

Expanding Your Sticker Business: Tips and Strategies

Once you have a solid foundation for your sticker business, you can explore various strategies to expand your reach and increase your revenue. Here are some tips to help you grow your business:

1. Diversify Your Product Offerings

- **Custom Stickers:** Offer custom sticker design and printing services to cater to individual needs.
- **Sticker Packs:** Create themed sticker packs to attract a wider audience.
- **Sticker Bundles:** Offer discounts on bulk purchases to encourage larger orders.
- **Limited Edition Stickers:** Release limited edition stickers to create a sense of urgency and exclusivity.

2. Expand Your Market Reach

- **Online Marketplaces:** Sell your stickers on popular online marketplaces like Etsy, Amazon, and Redbubble.
- **Social Media Marketing:** Utilize social media platforms to showcase your products and engage with your audience.
- **Influencer Partnerships:** Collaborate with influencers to promote your stickers to their followers.
- **Wholesale Partnerships:** Partner with retailers to distribute your stickers to a wider audience.

3. Enhance Your Brand

- **Consistent Branding:** Develop a strong brand identity and maintain consistency across all your marketing materials.
- **Storytelling:** Share your brand story to connect with your audience on an emotional level.
- **Customer Engagement:** Build a loyal customer base by providing excellent customer service and engaging with your audience.

4. Explore New Markets

- **International Market:** Expand your business to international markets by partnering with distributors or selling directly to customers in other countries.
- **Corporate Market:** Target corporate clients by offering custom branded stickers for employee incentives, promotional events, and product packaging.
- **Retail Partnerships:** Collaborate with retailers to sell your stickers in physical stores.

5. Continuous Innovation

- **Stay Updated:** Keep up with the latest trends and technologies in the sticker industry.
- **Experiment with New Materials and Techniques:** Try out new materials and techniques to create unique and innovative stickers.
- **Customer Feedback:** Listen to customer feedback and use it to improve your products and services.

By implementing these strategies, you can expand your sticker business and achieve long-term success.

Additional Considerations for Sticker Design and Production

Color and Design

- **Color Psychology:** Consider the psychological impact of colors on your target audience.
- **Simplicity:** Keep your designs simple and easy to understand.
- **Contrast:** Ensure good contrast between the background and foreground colors.
- **Font Choice:** Choose fonts that are easy to read and complement your brand.

Size and Shape

- **Purpose:** The size and shape of your sticker should be appropriate for its intended use.
- **Readability:** Ensure that the text and graphics are legible, even at smaller sizes.
- **Die-Cut Options:** Consider custom die-cut shapes to make your stickers more eye-catching.

Printing Techniques

- **Digital Printing:** Versatile and ideal for small quantities and custom designs.
- **Screen Printing:** Best for large quantities and bold, solid colors.
- **Offset Printing:** Cost-effective for large quantities and complex designs.

Packaging and Shipping

- **Protective Packaging:** Use appropriate packaging materials to protect your stickers during shipping.
- **Labeling:** Clearly label your packages to avoid confusion and damage.

- **Shipping Method:** Choose a reliable shipping method to ensure timely delivery.

Quality Control

- **Proofing:** Review proofs carefully to ensure accuracy in design, color, and size.
- **Quality Inspection:** Inspect the final product for any defects or imperfections.
- **Customer Feedback:** Gather feedback from customers to identify areas for improvement.

By carefully considering these factors, you can create high-quality stickers that will effectively promote your brand and leave a lasting impression.

Sticker Finishes and Laminations: A Deeper Dive

Sticker finishes and laminations play a crucial role in enhancing the appearance, durability, and overall impact of your stickers. By understanding the different options available, you can create custom stickers that are both visually appealing and functional.

Sticker Finishes

- **Matte Finish:**
    - Non-reflective surface
    - Ideal for text-heavy stickers and those with intricate designs
    - Provides a clean, professional look
- **Glossy Finish:**
    - Shiny, reflective surface
    - Enhances colors and images
    - Can be prone to fingerprints and smudges
- **Satin Finish:**
    - A balance between matte and glossy
    - Offers a subtle sheen without the glare of a glossy finish
    - Provides a more elegant and sophisticated look

Sticker Laminations

Laminating your stickers can add an extra layer of protection and enhance their overall appearance.

- **Matte Laminate:**
    - Protects the sticker from scratches and UV damage
    - Maintains the matte finish of the sticker
    - Ideal for stickers that need to be durable but retain a soft, matte look
- **Glossy Laminate:**
    - Protects the sticker from scratches and UV damage
    - Adds a high-gloss, shiny finish
    - Enhances the vibrancy of colors and images
- **UV Laminate:**

- Provides excellent protection against scratches, water, and UV damage
- Ideal for outdoor stickers and those that need to withstand harsh conditions

Choosing the Right Finish and Lamination

When selecting a finish and lamination for your stickers, consider the following factors:

- **Purpose:** What is the primary purpose of the sticker?
- **Target Audience:** Who is your target audience?
- **Budget:** What is your budget?
- **Aesthetic Appeal:** What look and feel do you want to achieve?
- **Durability:** How durable does the sticker need to be?

By carefully considering these factors, you can choose the right finish and lamination to create custom stickers that meet your specific needs and exceed your expectations.

Remember: The combination of sticker material, adhesive, cutting technique, finish, and lamination will ultimately determine the overall quality, durability, and aesthetic appeal of your stickers.

Ink and Color Management: A Deeper Dive

Ink: The Lifeblood of Printing

As we've discussed, ink is a critical component of the digital printing process. The type of ink used can significantly impact the final appearance, durability, and cost of a printed piece.

Key Ink Types and Their Applications:

- **Dye-based Inks:** Ideal for photo prints and other high-quality color prints. They offer vibrant colors but may fade over time, especially when exposed to light and moisture.
- **Pigment-Based Inks:** These inks are more durable and fade-resistant, making them suitable for outdoor signage, banners, and other long-lasting applications.
- **UV Curable Inks:** These inks cure instantly when exposed to UV light, resulting in highly durable and water-resistant prints. They're often used for packaging, labels, and other high-quality applications.
- **Latex Inks:** Environmentally friendly, low-odor inks that are ideal for indoor signage, posters, and canvas prints.

Color Management: Ensuring Accurate Color Reproduction

Color management is the process of ensuring consistent color reproduction across different devices and printing processes. It involves a combination of hardware, software, and techniques to achieve accurate color representation.

Key Factors in Color Management:

- **Monitor Calibration:** Calibrating your monitor ensures that the colors you see on screen accurately represent the final printed output.
- **Printer Profiles:** Printer profiles provide information about a specific printer's color capabilities, allowing for accurate color matching.

- **Proofing:** Proofing involves comparing a printed sample to a digital proof to identify any color discrepancies.
- **Ink and Paper:** The type of ink and paper used can significantly impact color reproduction.
- **Printing Settings:** Proper printing settings, such as ink density and color management, are crucial for accurate color output.

Color Gamut:

The color gamut refers to the range of colors that a particular device or printing process can reproduce. A wider color gamut allows for a broader range of colors, resulting in more vibrant and accurate prints.

Common Color Spaces:

- **sRGB:** A standard color space used for most digital displays and web graphics.
- **Adobe RGB:** A wider color gamut than sRGB, often used for photography and high-end printing.
- **CMYK:** A color model used in printing, combining cyan, magenta, yellow, and black inks.

By understanding the intricacies of ink and color management, you can produce high-quality printed materials that meet your specific needs and exceed your expectations.

Ink and Color Management: A Deeper Dive

Ink and Its Impact on Print Quality

The type of ink used can significantly influence the quality, durability, and overall appearance of a printed piece. Here are some key factors to consider:

- **Ink Type:** As discussed earlier, the choice of ink (dye-based, pigment-based, UV curable, or latex) depends on the specific application and desired outcome.
- **Ink Density:** The concentration of pigment in the ink affects the color intensity and overall print quality.
- **Ink Viscosity:** The viscosity of the ink influences its flow and application, impacting the sharpness of details and the smoothness of the print.

Color Management: Ensuring Accurate Color Reproduction

Color management is a critical aspect of digital printing, ensuring that colors are accurately reproduced from the digital design to the final printed output. Key factors influencing color accuracy include:

- **Monitor Calibration:** Calibrating your monitor ensures that the colors you see on screen accurately represent the printed colors.
- **Color Profiles:** Using the correct color profile (e.g., sRGB, Adobe RGB, CMYK) ensures consistent color reproduction across different devices and software.
- **Proofing:** Proofing your designs on a proof press or using a proof printer allows you to visually assess the color accuracy before final printing.
- **Ink and Paper Combinations:** The combination of ink and paper can affect color reproduction. Certain paper types may absorb ink differently, leading to variations in color.

Challenges in Color Management

- **Device Variations:** Different devices, such as monitors, printers, and scanners, may display colors differently.
- **Lighting Conditions:** Ambient lighting can affect how colors are perceived.
- **Human Perception:** Individual perception of color can vary.

Best Practices for Color Management

- **Regular Monitor Calibration:** Calibrate your monitor regularly to ensure accurate color representation.
- **Use High-Quality Color Profiles:** Use high-quality color profiles for both your monitor and printer.
- **Proofing:** Proof your designs before printing to verify color accuracy.
- **Control the Printing Environment:** Maintain consistent lighting conditions in your printing environment.
- **Choose the Right Paper:** Select paper that is compatible with your ink and desired color output.
- **Regular Maintenance:** Keep your printing equipment clean and well-maintained to ensure optimal performance.

By understanding the intricacies of ink and color management, you can produce high-quality prints that meet your clients' expectations and enhance your brand's image.

Specialty Papers: Elevating Your Print Projects

Specialty papers offer unique characteristics and can significantly enhance the visual appeal and tactile experience of your printed materials. Here are some popular specialty papers and their applications:

Metallic Papers

- **Shimmering Effect:** Creates a luxurious and eye-catching look.
- **Applications:** Packaging, invitations, business cards, and greeting cards.

Recycled Paper

- **Eco-Friendly:** Reduces environmental impact.
- **Applications:** Brochures, flyers, and business cards.

Vellum

- **Translucent:** Adds a delicate and elegant touch.
- **Applications:** Invitations, certificates, and menus.

Colored Paper

- **Vibrant Colors:** Adds a pop of color to your designs.
- **Applications:** Brochures, flyers, and business cards.

Textured Paper

- **Tactile Experience:** Creates a unique tactile sensation.
- **Applications:** Invitations, business cards, and packaging.

Embossed Paper

- **3D Effect:** Adds depth and dimension to your designs.
- **Applications:** Invitations, book covers, and packaging.

Debossing Paper

- **Subtle Design:** Creates a recessed design for a sophisticated look.
- **Applications:** Invitations, business cards, and packaging.

Choosing the Right Specialty Paper

When selecting a specialty paper, consider the following factors:

- **Purpose:** What is the primary purpose of the printed material?
- **Target Audience:** Who is your target audience?
- **Budget:** What is your budget?
- **Aesthetic Appeal:** What look and feel do you want to achieve?
- **Durability:** How durable does the printed material need to be?

By carefully selecting the right specialty paper, you can create stunning printed materials that will leave a lasting impression on your audience.

Paper Weight and Thickness: A Deeper Dive

As we've discussed, paper weight, measured in Grams Per Square Meter (GSM), significantly impacts the overall feel and quality of a printed piece. Here's a more detailed breakdown of common GSM ranges and their typical applications:

Lightweight Papers (60-90 GSM)

- **Newsprint:** A low-cost paper used for newspapers and basic printing.
- **Bond Paper:** A versatile paper used for office documents, letters, and envelopes.

Medium-Weight Papers (90-120 GSM)

- **Offset Paper:** A popular choice for magazines, brochures, and catalogs.
- **Book Paper:** Used for books, textbooks, and manuals.

Heavyweight Papers (120-170 GSM)

- **Cardstock:** A thick, sturdy paper used for business cards, postcards, and covers.
- **Cover Stock:** A heavier weight paper used for book covers, brochures, and folders.

Super Heavyweight Papers (170+ GSM)

- **Board:** A very thick paper used for packaging, boxes, and signage.

Factors Affecting Paper Weight and Thickness:

- **Fiber Content:** The type of fiber used (e.g., wood pulp, cotton) affects the paper's weight and texture.

- **Manufacturing Process:** The manufacturing process, including the amount of pressure and heat applied, can influence the paper's weight and thickness.
- **Paper Finish:** The paper's finish, such as matte, glossy, or textured, can also affect its weight and thickness.

Choosing the Right Paper Weight

When selecting a paper weight, consider the following factors:

- **Purpose:** What is the primary purpose of the printed material?
- **Durability:** How durable does the printed material need to be?
- **Aesthetic Appeal:** What look and feel do you want to achieve?
- **Print Quality:** The paper weight should be suitable for the desired print quality.
- **Cost:** The cost of paper varies based on its weight, finish, and specialty.

By carefully considering these factors, you can select the appropriate paper weight to create high-quality, visually appealing printed materials.

Paper Finishes and Textures: A Closer Look

Paper finishes and textures play a crucial role in the overall aesthetic appeal of printed materials. By understanding the different options available, you can create visually stunning and tactile experiences for your audience.

Common Paper Finishes

- **Matte:** A classic, non-reflective finish that is ideal for text-heavy documents, such as books, magazines, and brochures. It offers excellent print quality and readability.
- **Glossy:** A high-gloss finish that provides vibrant colors and sharp images. It's perfect for high-impact materials like brochures, flyers, and postcards.
- **Silk:** A balance between matte and glossy, offering a subtle sheen. It's a popular choice for a wide range of applications, including business cards, invitations, and packaging.
- **Uncoated:** A natural, textured finish that provides a rustic or vintage look. It's often used for eco-friendly printing and specialty paper products.

Paper Textures

- **Smooth:** A smooth, flat surface, ideal for high-resolution images and crisp text.
- **Textured:** A textured surface that adds depth and visual interest.
- **Embossed:** A textured surface created by pressing a design into the paper.
- **Debossing:** A recessed design created by pressing a design into the paper.

Specialty Papers

Specialty papers offer unique characteristics and can elevate the look and feel of your printed materials. Here are some popular specialty papers:

- **Colored Paper:** Available in a wide range of colors, colored paper can add a touch of personality to your designs.
- **Metallic Paper:** A paper with a metallic finish, often used for luxury packaging and invitations.
- **Recycled Paper:** An eco-friendly option that reduces environmental impact.
- **Vellum:** A translucent paper with a smooth, slightly textured surface, often used for certificates and invitations.
- **Cardstock:** A thick, sturdy paper, ideal for business cards, postcards, and packaging.

Choosing the Right Paper

When selecting paper for your project, consider the following factors:

- **Purpose:** What is the primary purpose of the printed material?
- **Target Audience:** Who is your target audience?
- **Budget:** What is your budget?
- **Aesthetic Appeal:** What look and feel do you want to achieve?
- **Durability:** How durable does the printed material need to be?

By carefully considering these factors and working closely with your printer, you can choose the right paper to create stunning printed materials that will leave a lasting impression.

Expanding Your Digital Printing Business

Once your digital printing business is well-established, you may consider expanding your operations to reach a wider market and increase revenue. Here are some strategies for expansion:

1. Geographic Expansion

- **Open New Locations:** Consider opening additional physical locations in new markets.
- **Online Expansion:** Expand your online presence to reach a global audience.
- **Partnerships:** Partner with local businesses in other regions to offer your services.

2. Product and Service Expansion

- **Diversify Product Offerings:** Expand your product line to include new items like custom apparel, home decor, and packaging.
- **Value-Added Services:** Offer additional services, such as design, finishing, and shipping.
- **Specialized Services:** Focus on niche markets, such as fine art printing or large-format printing.

3. Strategic Partnerships

- **Collaborate with Other Businesses:** Partner with complementary businesses, such as marketing agencies, event planners, and interior designers.
- **Joint Ventures:** Form joint ventures with other businesses to share resources and expertise.

4. Technology Adoption

- **Automation:** Implement automation tools to streamline operations and reduce costs.

- **E-commerce:** Invest in a robust e-commerce platform to sell your products online.
- **AI and Machine Learning:** Utilize AI and machine learning to improve efficiency and decision-making.

5. Customer Experience

- **Personalized Service:** Offer personalized services to build strong customer relationships.
- **Loyalty Programs:** Implement loyalty programs to reward repeat customers.
- **Excellent Customer Support:** Provide exceptional customer support to address customer inquiries and concerns promptly.

6. Financial Planning

- **Secure Funding:** Explore funding options, such as loans, investments, or crowdfunding.
- **Financial Forecasting:** Create detailed financial forecasts to plan for future growth.
- **Risk Management:** Identify and mitigate potential risks, such as economic downturns and supply chain disruptions.

By carefully considering these expansion strategies and implementing a solid business plan, you can position your digital printing business for sustained growth and success.

Building a Strong Team

A strong team is essential for the success of any business, especially in a dynamic industry like digital printing. Here are some tips for building a talented and motivated team:

1. Hire the Right People

- **Clear Job Descriptions:** Create detailed job descriptions outlining the specific skills and experience required for each position.
- **Effective Interviewing:** Conduct thorough interviews to assess candidates' qualifications, skills, and cultural fit.
- **Skills and Personality:** Look for individuals with strong technical skills, creativity, problem-solving abilities, and a positive attitude.

2. Foster a Positive Work Environment

- **Open Communication:** Encourage open and honest communication among team members.
- **Employee Recognition:** Recognize and reward employees for their contributions.
- **Professional Development:** Provide opportunities for training and development.
- **Work-Life Balance:** Promote a healthy work-life balance.

3. Empower Your Team

- **Delegate Authority:** Empower employees to make decisions and take ownership of their work.
- **Provide Feedback:** Offer constructive feedback to help employees improve.
- **Set Clear Expectations:** Clearly communicate expectations and goals.

4. Leadership and Mentorship

- **Strong Leadership:** Lead by example and inspire your team.
- **Mentorship:** Mentor team members to help them grow and develop.
- **Collaboration:** Foster a collaborative and supportive team culture.

5. Employee Retention

- **Competitive Compensation:** Offer competitive salaries and benefits.
- **Career Advancement Opportunities:** Provide opportunities for career growth and advancement.
- **Positive Company Culture:** Create a positive and inclusive work environment.

By investing in your team, you can create a high-performing organization that will drive your business forward.

Additional Considerations for a Successful Digital Printing Business

While a solid business plan is essential, there are several other factors to consider for long-term success in the digital printing industry:

1. Environmental Sustainability

- **Eco-Friendly Practices:** Implement eco-friendly practices, such as using recycled paper, energy-efficient equipment, and soy-based inks.
- **Waste Reduction:** Minimize waste by optimizing production processes and recycling materials.
- **Certifications:** Obtain certifications like FSC (Forest Stewardship Council) and ISO 14001 to demonstrate your commitment to sustainability.

2. Customer Service Excellence

- **Responsive Customer Support:** Provide prompt and effective customer support to build trust and loyalty.
- **Personalized Service:** Offer personalized solutions to meet the unique needs of each customer.
- **High-Quality Products:** Deliver high-quality products that exceed customer expectations.

3. Continuous Innovation

- **Stay Updated:** Keep up with the latest trends and technologies in the industry.
- **Experiment with New Products and Services:** Offer innovative products and services to attract new customers.
- **Collaborate with Other Businesses:** Partner with complementary businesses to expand your offerings.

4. Risk Management

- **Identify Risks:** Assess potential risks, such as economic downturns, supply chain disruptions, and equipment failures.
- **Develop Contingency Plans:** Create contingency plans to mitigate risks and minimize their impact.
- **Insurance:** Obtain adequate insurance coverage to protect your business from unforeseen events.

5. Financial Management

- **Cash Flow Management:** Monitor your cash flow closely to ensure you have enough funds to meet your obligations.
- **Financial Forecasting:** Create detailed financial forecasts to plan for future growth.
- **Cost Control:** Implement cost-cutting measures to improve profitability.

6. Legal and Regulatory Compliance

- **Business Licenses and Permits:** Obtain all necessary licenses and permits.
- **Intellectual Property:** Protect your intellectual property, such as trademarks and copyrights.
- **Tax Compliance:** Stay compliant with all tax laws and regulations.

By carefully considering these additional factors, you can build a successful and sustainable digital printing business.

Leveraging Technology for Efficiency and Growth

In today's digital age, technology plays a crucial role in the success of any business, including digital printing. By leveraging technology, you can streamline operations, improve efficiency, and enhance customer satisfaction.

Key Technologies to Consider:

- **Design Software:** Invest in powerful design software to create professional-quality designs.
- **Print Management Software:** Utilize print management software to streamline your workflow and reduce errors.
- **E-commerce Platform:** Set up an online store to sell your products and services directly to customers.
- **Customer Relationship Management (CRM) Software:** Manage customer interactions and track sales.
- **Cloud-Based Storage:** Store your files securely in the cloud to access them from anywhere.
- **Automation Tools:** Automate repetitive tasks to save time and reduce human error.

Benefits of Technology:

- **Increased Efficiency:** Automation and streamlined workflows can significantly improve productivity.
- **Improved Accuracy:** Technology can help reduce errors and ensure consistency in your products.
- **Enhanced Customer Experience:** Offer online ordering, real-time tracking, and personalized services.
- **Data-Driven Decision Making:** Analyze data to make informed business decisions.
- **Scalability:** Technology allows you to scale your business and meet growing demand.

Staying Updated with Technology Trends

The digital printing industry is constantly evolving. To stay ahead of the curve, it's important to:

- **Attend Industry Events:** Network with other professionals and learn about the latest trends.
- **Subscribe to Industry Publications:** Stay informed about industry news and best practices.
- **Continuous Learning:** Invest in training and development to acquire new skills and knowledge.
- **Embrace Emerging Technologies:** Explore technologies like artificial intelligence, machine learning, and augmented reality to gain a competitive edge.

By embracing technology and staying updated with the latest trends, you can position your niche digital printing business for long-term success.

Financial Considerations for a Niche Digital Printing Business

Financial planning is a critical aspect of starting and running a successful digital printing business. Here are some key financial considerations:

Startup Costs:

- **Equipment:** Invest in high-quality printing equipment, such as printers, cutters, laminators, and software.
- **Supplies:** Purchase paper, ink, and other supplies.
- **Business License and Permits:** Obtain necessary licenses and permits to operate your business legally.
- **Marketing and Advertising:** Allocate funds for marketing and advertising to attract customers.
- **Rent and Utilities:** Consider the costs of renting a workspace or setting up a home-based business.
- **Insurance:** Protect your business with appropriate insurance coverage.

Ongoing Costs:

- **Supplies:** Continuously purchase paper, ink, and other supplies.
- **Maintenance and Repairs:** Allocate funds for equipment maintenance and repairs.
- **Software Licenses and Updates:** Keep your software up-to-date.
- **Utilities:** Pay for electricity, water, and internet.
- **Rent or Mortgage:** If you have a physical location, pay rent or mortgage.
- **Employee Salaries and Benefits:** If you hire employees, pay their salaries and benefits.
- **Marketing and Advertising:** Continue to invest in marketing and advertising to maintain brand visibility.

Pricing Strategy:

- **Cost-Based Pricing:** Calculate your costs, including materials, labor, and overhead, and add a markup to determine your price.
- **Value-Based Pricing:** Base your prices on the perceived value of your products and services.
- **Competitive Pricing:** Research your competitors' pricing and adjust your prices accordingly.

Financial Management:

- **Accounting and Bookkeeping:** Maintain accurate financial records.
- **Cash Flow Management:** Monitor your cash flow to ensure you have enough funds to meet your obligations.
- **Tax Planning:** Consult with a tax professional to minimize your tax liability.
- **Financial Forecasting:** Create financial forecasts to plan for future growth and challenges.

Seeking Financial Assistance:

- **Small Business Loans:** Explore options for small business loans from banks or credit unions.
- **Grants:** Research government grants and other funding opportunities for small businesses.
- **Crowdfunding:** Consider crowdfunding platforms to raise capital from a large number of people.
- **Investors:** Seek investment from angel investors or venture capitalists.

By carefully considering these financial factors, you can make informed decisions and ensure the long-term success of your niche digital printing business.

Niche Specialization: A Deeper Dive

Niche specialization allows you to stand out in a crowded market. By focusing on a specific area, you can develop a strong reputation, attract loyal customers, and charge premium prices. Here are some strategies to further specialize your niche:

- **Sub-Niche:** Consider further subdividing your niche to target a more specific audience. For example, if you're in the wedding invitation niche, you could specialize in eco-friendly invitations or destination wedding invitations.
- **Unique Selling Proposition (USP):** Identify what sets you apart from your competitors. This could be your expertise, unique printing techniques, or exceptional customer service.
- **Partnerships:** Collaborate with complementary businesses to expand your offerings and reach a wider audience. For instance, partner with a wedding planner or event organizer to offer bundled packages.
- **Continuous Learning:** Stay updated on the latest trends, technologies, and industry best practices. Attend industry conferences, workshops, and webinars to enhance your skills and knowledge.

Marketing Your Niche Business

Effective marketing is crucial for attracting and retaining customers in a niche market. Here are some marketing strategies to consider:

- **Digital Marketing:**
    - **SEO:** Optimize your website for search engines to attract organic traffic.
    - **Social Media Marketing:** Use social media platforms to connect with your target audience and share valuable content.
    - **Content Marketing:** Create high-quality content, such as blog posts, articles, and videos, to establish your expertise and attract potential customers.

- **Email Marketing:** Build an email list and send regular newsletters to keep your customers engaged.
- **Traditional Marketing:**
  - **Print Advertising:** Use print advertising, such as flyers, brochures, and business cards, to reach your target audience.
  - **Local Partnerships:** Partner with local businesses, such as wedding planners, event organizers, and interior designers, to cross-promote your services.
- **Networking:** Attend industry events, join professional organizations, and network with other business owners to build relationships and generate referrals.

Building Strong Customer Relationships

Building strong relationships with your customers is essential for long-term success. Here are some tips for fostering customer loyalty:

- **Exceptional Customer Service:** Provide excellent customer service, from the initial consultation to the final delivery.
- **Personalized Service:** Tailor your services to the specific needs of each customer.
- **After-Sales Service:** Offer after-sales support, such as troubleshooting and maintenance.
- **Loyalty Programs:** Implement loyalty programs to reward repeat customers.
- **Positive Reviews:** Encourage satisfied customers to leave positive reviews on your website and social media channels.

By focusing on your niche, implementing effective marketing strategies, and building strong customer relationships, you can establish a successful and profitable digital printing business.

Career Opportunities in Digital Printing

The growth of digital printing has created a wide range of career opportunities for individuals with diverse skills and interests. Here are some of the career paths you can explore in the digital printing industry:

- **Graphic Designer:** Create visually appealing designs for various print materials, such as brochures, flyers, and packaging.
- **Pre-Press Technician:** Prepare digital files for printing, ensuring accurate color reproduction and optimal print quality.
- **Print Operator:** Operate digital printing machines and monitor the printing process to ensure high-quality output.
- **Color Management Specialist:** Manage color consistency and accuracy throughout the printing process.
- **Sales and Marketing Representative:** Sell printing services to clients and build strong relationships with customers.
- **Business Owner:** Start your own digital printing business, offering a range of printing services to clients.

To succeed in the digital printing industry, it's essential to stay updated on the latest trends and technologies. Continuous learning and skill development are crucial to remain competitive in this rapidly evolving field.

Conclusion

Digital printing has revolutionized the way we print, offering numerous benefits such as faster turnaround times, lower costs, and greater flexibility. As technology continues to advance, the future of digital printing looks bright. By embracing sustainable practices and innovative technologies, the printing industry can continue to grow while minimizing its environmental impact.

Environmental Impact of Digital Printing

While digital printing offers numerous benefits, it's important to consider its environmental impact. Traditional printing methods often involve the use of harmful chemicals and generate significant waste. However, digital printing has the potential to be more environmentally friendly.

Reducing Environmental Impact:

- **Energy Efficiency:** Digital printing often requires less energy than traditional printing methods, especially for short-run jobs.
- **Reduced Waste:** Digital printing minimizes waste by eliminating the need for large print runs and excess materials.
- **Sustainable Materials:** Many digital printing companies are adopting eco-friendly practices, such as using recycled paper and soy-based inks.
- **Water Conservation:** Digital printing processes typically use less water than traditional methods.

Challenges and Future Directions:

Despite its environmental advantages, digital printing still faces challenges:

- **Energy Consumption:** While digital printing is more energy-efficient than traditional methods, it still requires significant energy to power the equipment.
- **Electronic Waste:** The disposal of old printers and other digital printing equipment can contribute to electronic waste.
- **Chemical Use:** Although digital printing uses fewer chemicals than traditional methods, some chemicals are still involved in the printing process.

To address these challenges, the printing industry is exploring innovative solutions:

- **Energy-Efficient Equipment:** Developing more energy-efficient printers and other equipment.
- **Recycling and Reuse:** Implementing recycling programs for paper, ink cartridges, and other materials.
- **Sustainable Materials:** Using eco-friendly materials, such as recycled paper and biodegradable inks.
- **Green Certifications:** Obtaining certifications that recognize environmentally responsible practices.

By adopting sustainable practices and investing in innovative technologies, the digital printing industry can continue to grow while minimizing its environmental impact.

The Impact of Digital Printing on Society

Digital printing has not only transformed the printing industry but has also had a significant impact on society as a whole. Here are some of the ways digital printing has shaped our world:

- **Education:** Digital printing has revolutionized the way educational materials are produced. It has made it easier to create customized textbooks, workbooks, and other learning materials. Additionally, digital printing has enabled the production of low-cost, high-quality educational materials, making education more accessible to people around the world.
- **Healthcare:** Digital printing has played a crucial role in the healthcare industry, enabling the production of personalized medical devices, prosthetics, and drug delivery systems. It has also facilitated the creation of high-quality medical images and diagnostic tools.
- **Art and Design:** Digital printing has empowered artists and designers to bring their creative visions to life. It has made it easier to experiment with different materials, colors, and textures, leading to the creation of stunning and innovative works of art.
- **Marketing and Advertising:** Digital printing has transformed the way businesses market their products and services. It has enabled the creation of high-quality

marketing materials, such as brochures, flyers, and posters, at a fraction of the cost of traditional printing methods.

The Future of Digital Printing

As technology continues to advance, the future of digital printing looks even more promising. Some of the exciting trends in digital printing include:

- **3D Printing:** 3D printing is a revolutionary technology that allows the creation of three-dimensional objects from digital models. This technology has the potential to transform industries such as manufacturing, healthcare, and construction.
- **Flexible Electronics:** Digital printing can be used to print electronic circuits on flexible materials, such as plastic and fabric. This technology has applications in wearable technology, smart packaging, and medical devices.
- **Personalized Products:** Digital printing enables the mass customization of products, allowing consumers to create personalized items that reflect their individual tastes and preferences.

In conclusion, digital printing has had a profound impact on our society. It has made our lives easier, more efficient, and more creative. As technology continues to evolve, we can expect to see even more innovative and exciting applications of digital printing in the years to come.

Glossary of Printing Terms

A

- **CMYK:** A color model used in printing, combining cyan, magenta, yellow, and black inks.
- **DPI:** Dots Per Inch, a measure of image resolution.
- **DPS:** Dots Per Square Inch, a measure of print resolution.

B

- **Bleed:** Extending the image beyond the trim edge to ensure full coverage after trimming.
- **Binding:** The process of attaching pages together to form a book or booklet.
- **Brochure:** A printed document that typically consists of multiple folded pages.

C

- **Color Profile:** A standardized set of data that defines a specific color space.
- **Color Separation:** The process of separating a color image into individual color channels.
- **CTP:** Computer-to-Plate, a technology that directly transfers digital images to printing plates.

D

- **Die-Cutting:** Cutting paper or cardstock into custom shapes.
- **DPI:** Dots Per Inch, a measure of image resolution.
- **DPS:** Dots Per Square Inch, a measure of print resolution.

E

- **Embossing:** Raising a design on the surface of paper or cardstock.

- **Encapsulation:** Sealing a printed piece in plastic to protect it from damage.

F

- **File Format:** The structure and organization of a digital file.
- **Finishing:** The final processes applied to a printed product, such as folding, trimming, and binding.
- **Foil Stamping:** Applying metallic or colored foil to a printed surface.

G

- **Gamut:** The range of colors that a particular device or printing process can reproduce.
- **Glossy:** A shiny paper finish.
- **Grain Direction:** The direction of the paper fibers, which can affect the appearance of the printed image.

H

- **Halftone:** A technique used to reproduce continuous-tone images using dots of varying size.

I

- **Inkjet Printing:** A digital printing process that sprays tiny droplets of ink onto a surface.
- **ISO Standards:** International standards for paper sizes and printing processes.

L

- **Laser Printing:** A digital printing process that uses a laser beam to create an image on a drum.
- **Layout:** The arrangement of elements on a printed page.
- **Lamination:** Applying a plastic film to the surface of a printed product to protect it.

M

- **Matte:** A non-glossy paper finish.
- **Mockup:** A physical or digital representation of a printed product.

O

- **Offset Printing:** A traditional printing technique that involves transferring ink from a plate to a rubber blanket, and then onto the paper.
- **Opacity:** The ability of paper to block light and prevent show-through.

P

- **PMS:** Pantone Matching System, a standardized color matching system.
- **Proof:** A sample print used to evaluate color accuracy and overall quality.
- **Punching:** Creating holes in paper for binding or other purposes.

R

- **Resolution:** The number of pixels per inch in a digital image.
- **RGB:** A color model used in digital displays, combining red, green, and blue colors.

S

- **Screen Printing:** A printing technique that uses a mesh screen to transfer ink onto a substrate.
- **Saddle Stitching:** A binding method that involves stapling the pages of a booklet.
- **Spot UV:** Applying a glossy coating to specific areas of a printed piece.

T

- **Toner:** A fine powder used in laser and toner printers.
- **Trim Size:** The final size of a printed piece after trimming.

V

- **Varnish:** A protective coating applied to the surface of a printed product.
- **Vector Graphics:** Images created using mathematical equations, which can be scaled without losing quality.

This glossary provides a basic overview of common printing terms. For more specific definitions and explanations, consult industry-specific resources and reference materials.

Resources and Suppliers for Digital Printing

Online Resources and Communities:

- **Print Industry Professionals Association (PIPA):** A global network of printing professionals.
- **Printing Industries of America (PIA):** Provides resources, education, and advocacy for the printing industry.
- **SGIA:** Specializes in specialty graphic imaging and printing.
- **Printing Forums and Communities:** Online forums like Reddit and specialized printing forums where you can connect with other printers, ask questions, and share experiences.

Suppliers of Printing Equipment and Supplies:

- **Xerox:** Offers a wide range of digital printing equipment and supplies.
- **HP:** Provides high-quality printers and inks for various applications.
- **Canon:** Manufactures a variety of digital printing solutions.
- **Konica Minolta:** Offers digital printing systems for commercial printing.
- **Paper Suppliers:**
    - **Paper Mart:** Offers a wide range of paper types and sizes.
    - **Specialty Paper:** Provides specialty papers for unique projects.
    - **Fastenal:** Offers industrial and commercial supplies, including paper products.
- **Ink and Toner Suppliers:**
    - **Office Depot/OfficeMax:** Offers a variety of ink and toner options.
    - **Amazon:** A convenient online marketplace for purchasing ink and toner.
- **Finishing Equipment Suppliers:**
    - **MBO:** Offers a range of finishing equipment, including folders, binders, and cutters.

- o **Horizon:** Provides high-quality finishing equipment for commercial printers.

Software and Design Tools:

- **Adobe Creative Suite:** Industry-standard software for graphic design, photo editing, and illustration.
- **CorelDRAW Graphics Suite:** Versatile graphic design software for various design tasks.
- **Affinity Designer and Photo:** Professional-grade design software.
- **Canva:** User-friendly design tool for creating social media graphics, presentations, and more.

By utilizing these resources and suppliers, you can ensure that your digital printing business has access to the latest technology, quality supplies, and expert support.

Sample Business Plan: Digital Printing Business

Executive Summary

XYZ LLC, is a digital printing business that offers a wide range of printing services, including business cards, flyers, posters, brochures, and custom apparel. Our goal is to provide high-quality, affordable, and timely printing solutions to our customers.

We will leverage state-of-the-art digital printing technology to deliver exceptional results. Our target market includes small businesses, organizations, and individuals.

Company Description

XYZ LLC is a Your Legal Structure, e.g., LLC, Corporation based in Your City, State. Our mission is to provide top-notch printing services that exceed customer expectations. Our experienced team is dedicated to delivering high-quality products and outstanding customer service.

Market Analysis

The digital printing industry is experiencing significant growth due to advancements in technology and increasing demand for personalized products. Our target market includes:

- **Small Businesses:** Need high-quality printed materials for marketing and branding.
- **Organizations:** Require professional-looking printed materials for events and promotions.
- **Individuals:** Seek personalized products like custom t-shirts and photo prints.

Marketing and Sales Strategy

- **Digital Marketing:** Utilize SEO, social media, and email marketing to reach a wider audience.
- **Local Partnerships:** Collaborate with local businesses and organizations to generate referrals.
- **Customer Loyalty Programs:** Implement loyalty programs to reward repeat customers.
- **Networking:** Attend industry events and conferences to build relationships with potential clients.

Operations Plan

- **Equipment:** Invest in high-quality digital printing equipment, including printers, cutters, and laminators.
- **Software:** Utilize design software, RIP software, and other relevant software.
- **Supplies:** Source reliable suppliers for paper, ink, and other materials.
- **Workflow:** Establish efficient workflows to streamline production and reduce turnaround time.
- **Quality Control:** Implement strict quality control measures to ensure consistent product quality.

Financial Projections

Include detailed financial projections, such as income statements, balance sheets, and cash flow statements. Consider factors like startup costs, operating expenses, revenue projections, and break-even analysis.

Management Team

- **John Doe:** Your Role and Experience
- **Salina Doe :** Their Role and Experience
- **Morina Doe:** Their Role and Experience

Conclusion

XYZ LLC is well-positioned to succeed in the competitive digital printing industry. With a strong focus on quality, customer service, and innovation, we aim to establish ourselves as a leading provider of digital printing solutions.

Financial Projections for a Digital Printing Business

Note: These are projected figures and may vary based on specific business models, location, and market conditions. It's crucial to conduct thorough market research and consult with financial experts to create accurate projections.

Startup Costs

- **Equipment:** Printers, computers, software, finishing equipment (e.g., cutters, laminators, binders)
- **Supplies:** Paper, ink, toner, and other consumables
- **Rent or Lease:** For a physical location or warehouse
- **Utilities:** Electricity, water, internet
- **Insurance:** General liability, property, and workers' compensation
- **Licenses and Permits:** Business license, sales tax permit, and other required permits
- **Marketing and Advertising:** Website development, social media marketing, and print advertising
- **Legal and Accounting Fees:** For setting up the business and handling legal and financial matters

Ongoing Costs

- **Supplies:** Continuous purchase of paper, ink, and other consumables
- **Equipment Maintenance:** Regular maintenance and repairs for printers and other equipment
- **Software Licenses and Updates:** Keeping software up-to-date
- **Rent or Lease:** Ongoing costs for your physical location
- **Utilities:** Electricity, water, and internet
- **Insurance:** Regular payments for insurance premiums
- **Marketing and Advertising:** Ongoing costs for marketing and advertising campaigns
- **Employee Salaries and Benefits:** If applicable, salaries, taxes, and benefits for employees

- **Accounting and Taxes:** Fees for accounting services and tax preparation

Revenue Projections

- **Sales Revenue:** Estimate revenue from various services, such as printing business cards, flyers, posters, brochures, and custom apparel.
- **Service Revenue:** Revenue from additional services like design, finishing, and shipping.

Profit and Loss Statement

Item	Month 1	Month 2	Month 3	...	Annual Total
Revenue					
Sales Revenue					
Service Revenue					
Total Revenue					
Expenses					
Cost of Goods Sold (COGS)					
Salaries and Wages					
Rent/Lease					
Utilities					
Marketing and Advertising					
Insurance					
Legal and Accounting Fees					
Other Expenses					
Total Expenses					
Net Income/Loss					

Cash Flow Statement

- **Cash Inflows:** Sales revenue, loan proceeds, investments.
- **Cash Outflows:** Operating expenses, capital expenditures, debt payments.

Break-Even Analysis

- **Calculate Fixed Costs:** Rent, utilities, salaries, insurance, etc.
- **Calculate Variable Costs:** Cost of goods sold, shipping, and other variable expenses.
- **Determine Revenue Per Unit:** Average revenue generated per unit sold.
- **Calculate Break-Even Point:** The number of units you need to sell to cover your costs.

Remember to:

- **Consult with a Financial Advisor:** Seek expert advice to refine your financial projections.
- **Monitor and Adjust:** Regularly review and adjust your financial projections as needed.
- **Contingency Planning:** Develop a contingency plan to address unexpected challenges.

By carefully analyzing your financial projections, you can make informed decisions about your business and take steps to ensure its long-term success.

Conclusion

As you embark on your journey into the world of digital printing, remember that the key to success lies in a blend of technical expertise, creative vision, and a keen understanding of your customers' needs. By mastering the fundamentals of digital printing, exploring innovative techniques, and staying abreast of industry trends, you can build a thriving business that leaves a lasting impression.

Whether you're a seasoned professional or a budding entrepreneur, this book has provided you with a comprehensive guide to the intricacies of digital printing. From understanding paper types and ink technologies to mastering design software and color management, you've gained the knowledge to excel in this dynamic field.

As technology continues to evolve, so too will the possibilities of digital printing. By embracing innovation and staying adaptable, you can position yourself at the forefront of this exciting industry. Remember, the future of printing is in your hands.

www.ingramcontent.com/pod-product-compliance
Lightning Source LLC
Chambersburg PA
CBHW071036240526
45469CB00006BD/2228